As someone whose ministry is prayer mobilization, I have read hundreds of books on prayer in the last twenty years. None is better than *Extreme Prayer*. It is an easy read that combines inspirational stories with practical instruction. And as chairman of the board for Pioneer Bible Translators, I've been able to observe up close that Greg really does believe that "prayer is the strategy."

DAVE BUTTS
President, Harvest Prayer Ministries; chairman, America's National Prayer Committee

When I was asked to read Greg Pruett's book, I was almost reluctant to do so because books about prayer tend to make me feel guilty. *Great,* I thought, *let the guilt trip begin.* But the next several hours of reading were filled with African adventures, stories of miraculous healings, and some amazingly fresh insights into the sheer beauty of tenacious prayer. Read this book and you will learn that prayer is as much about listening as it is about speaking and as much about courage as it is about faith. *Extreme Prayer* will enable you to unleash the power that God desires to display in your life.

DREW SHERMAN
Lead pastor, Compass Christian Church, Colleyville, Texas

Extreme Prayer is a short, readable guide to taking your prayer life to a higher level. Drawing on his experience as a Bible translator and missionary, Greg marries solid biblical exposition to some interesting stories from his life on the mission field. Even more appealing is that Greg writes from the perspective of a Christian man who wants to know God better and to align his life with the will and Kingdom of God. His manuscript inspired a sermon series that was a great blessing to our church.

DR. BARRY McCARTY
Senior pastor, Peachtree Christian Church, Atlanta

God has seasoned Greg and his family for the greater service of getting his Word to the poor and illiterate people of the world. This book is a wonderful blend of Scripture and authentic personal experiences. As I read, I kept thinking, *Yep, that's how it has worked for me. He knows what he's talking about!*

GERALD A. JACKSON
President and founder, Hosanna/Faith Comes by Hearing; author, *Get God's Word to Every Person*

Brilliant! This book ignited a fire in me that had nearly been extinguished. It inspired me to follow a path I knew all along but that had nearly become overgrown. Thank you, Greg, for sharing your adventure with us.

HARRIET HILL, PHD
Trauma Healing Institute program director, American Bible Society; coauthor, *Healing the Wounds of Trauma: How the Church Can Help*

God wants to conform us to the image in which he created us—the image of God. In this brief but poignant book, my friend Greg Pruett shows how God, through Jesus' instructions and example, accomplishes that conformation. Becoming what God intended us to be is the purpose of our walk with Christ. The secret to that walk is ACTIVE prayer, which Greg takes to the *extreme*.

R. DANIEL SHAW
Professor of anthropology and translation, School of Intercultural Studies, Fuller Theological Seminary

EXTREME
PRAYER

The Impossible Prayers God Promises to Answer

GREG PRUETT

TYNDALE®
MOMENTUM

An Imprint of
Tyndale House Publishers, Inc.

Visit Tyndale online at www.tyndale.com.

Visit Tyndale Momentum online at www.tyndalemomentum.com.

TYNDALE, *Tyndale Momentum*, and the Tyndale Momentum logo are registered trademarks of Tyndale House Publishers, Inc. Tyndale Momentum is an imprint of Tyndale House Publishers, Inc.

Extreme Prayer: The Impossible Prayers God Promises to Answer

Designed by Ron Kaufmann

Library of Congress Cataloging-in-Publication Data

Pruett, Greg.
  Extreme prayer : the impossible prayers God promises to answer / Greg Pruett.
    pages cm
  Includes bibliographical references.
  ISBN 978-1-4143-8624-9 (hc)
  1. Prayer—Christianity. I. Title.
  BV220.P78 2014
  248.3′2—dc23   2013034042

Printed in the United States of America

20	19	18	17	16	15
8	7	6	5	4	3

I dedicate this book to the men, women, and children of Pioneer Bible Translators, who faithfully serve Bible-less peoples. They leave behind self-interest, and they risk their lives every day so that others will experience the transforming power of God's Word in their own language. They alternate between laughing together like family and weeping in loneliness because they miss their homelands and loved ones.

Some walk through steaming jungles and take motorized canoes just to get to their homes. They dig water wells for their families. At times they lie awake for hours, sweating through the night as they ache for the comfort of air-conditioning. I've seen others eagerly move their families to the frozen Arctic to make sure that, even there, none will lack Scripture. Still others have fled in the face of war, not merely to protect their lives, but so that they may later return to the field and serve again.

It is the great privilege and honor of my life to work alongside these ordinary people with extraordinary vision. I am always amazed at how joyfully they struggle to see the Word impact the lives of the Bible-less peoples around them. The world is not worthy of them (see Hebrews 11:38).

Contents

Foreword

MY OFFICE WINDOW overlooks a busy avenue. At any point during the day, I can witness a steady flow of traffic. Though I know little, if anything, about the driver of each car, this much I can assume. He or she has gassed up the tank. Each one has paused long enough in front of a gas pump to refuel. No gas means no power.

Can't the same be said about prayer? A stream of individuals passes through your world. Some of them accelerate with little or no effort. Many of them, however, are huffing and puffing. Their tanks are empty and their load is heavy.

They need some power. They need some prayer.

Oh, but prayer is such a puzzle. Why would God listen to me? Why do my thoughts matter to him? Do my prayers have an impact on his eternal plan?

My friend Greg Pruett says yes! We can be grateful that he has compiled his thoughts on prayer in this extremely helpful volume. I cannot recommend it enough.

I cannot recommend Greg enough either. I have

known him for over a quarter of a century. When my wife and I moved to San Antonio from Brazil in 1988, his family met us at the airport. I have served with his parents in leadership, worship, and outreach. I have seen Greg grow into one of the most effective leaders of our generation. He is trained as an engineer, linguist, and Bible teacher. He currently serves as the president of Pioneer Bible Translators, a vibrant ministry that is committed to translating the Bible into the language of Bible-less people groups around the world.

Greg, his wife, Rebecca, and the entire PBT team are teaching us the power of a ministry built on prayer. During the recent economic recession, when other ministries struggled, PBT flourished! When others were losing ground, they gained ground. Why? Their answer is this: prayer. Specific, continual, radical prayer.

God is using them to remind us . . . *Gas up the tank! Come to* me *for power! Enough relying on natural strength— lean into my supernatural, high-octane energy.*

Do yourself a favor and read this book! Let Greg mentor you into a new era of strength.

Greg, thanks for writing this book!

God, thanks for giving this book!

May we put it to use.

Max Lucado
AUGUST 2013

Shaken but Not Stirred

Extreme Prayer Begins with Need

THE INTENSITY OF the sun almost forced me back into the shelter of my West African home, but I was too focused on my stinging heart to feel the burn on my skin. Puffs of dust marked my pace as I stormed out of the village, across the road, and down the footpath leading to the jungle. That was it! My ministry was over; my marriage, finished. I was done. Like some kind of missionary recluse, I would stalk off into the bush and never return.

Silence gradually dominated the scrubby trail as I distanced myself from home. Only the drone of a passing bug or the cry of an occasional bird disturbed the still heat of the day. But inside, I was far from quiet. I angrily challenged God, *You did this to me!*

After all, he was the one who had wooed me into following this crazy dream to minister to a culture that had just one tiny, struggling church in an ocean of people who had never understood Jesus, never even heard that God loved them. Here I had given my life to him and settled into a small African village with only a few dozen known Christians to translate the Bible among a people who treasured the Qur'an as their holy book. I had planned to live for decades in this place and to help this people get the Word of God in their language. I wanted to help the small group of Christians multiply until every nearby village had a church. I had so hoped to make God proud of my life.

As I tromped down the path to nowhere, I interrogated God. *How could you let our mission die from such a basic thing as failure to live at peace with my wife?* I thought about how our screaming baby had robbed us of sleep. I ruminated over how we had fallen into a sleep-deprived pattern of shouting at each other.

Daytime had been no more peaceful. For weeks carpenters had been building a ceiling in our home, handcrafting every board from felled trees in the forest. We could find no place of refuge from the deafening pounding. On top of that, we had no running water or washing machine, so hand-washing cloth diapers absorbed much of our energy. It just didn't seem worth staying when we were investing all our time in survival instead of making progress on the mission.

By now, everyone in the village had to know we were collapsing under the weight of our dreams. If they had known English, anyone within an echo of our home would have heard us decide not only to quit the mission but also to go straight home and get a divorce. We might have actually left the mission field by now if we hadn't been so far from the airport. That monumental trek across hard roads may have been the last thing holding us back. We were teetering on the edge, and I just couldn't face it anymore. I had walked off into the bush swearing I would never come back, picturing myself as the next Tarzan, all the while grumbling to myself and to God.

Hours of sweaty miles later, I wasn't walking quite so fast. I began to face the prospect of my first night exposed to the swarming cloud of mosquitoes. What about the deadly green mambas that slithered in the dark? My resolve began to sink with the sun. Just as I started having second thoughts about life as a jungle hermit and began estimating how far I had wandered from home, I heard cars again. It suddenly dawned on me that my Tarzan career had been cut tragically short for lack of a GPS. I had turned on the wrong trail and walked a vast circle back to the highway that ran by our house. I felt like Jonah heaved up on some beach near Nineveh. God just wouldn't let me go. As it grew dark, I slunk back into the frosty atmosphere of the house without a word. I didn't tell Rebecca about my Tarzan act.

In desperation, we decided to grasp at one last-chance, lifesaving branch before sliding completely over the emotional cliff. We dedicated one week to go cry out to God in a cabin in the mountains. Could God fix the mess we had become? No sooner had we arrived at our prayer retreat than the baby came down with mumps and Rebecca became ill with some anonymous tropical plague. All week long, the baby wailed and Rebecca ailed. I just tried to nurse them both back to health. We did finally pray, but it was mostly on the way home in the car.

We decided to grasp at one last-chance, lifesaving branch before sliding completely over the emotional cliff.

Even though we had been too beaten down to manage much coherent prayer, God honored our decision to pray instead of giving up. He carefully considered our "groans that words cannot express" (Romans 8:26). In fact, Rebecca and I both point to that week as the turning point of our married lives and of our ministry. I remember talking and praying excitedly on our way home from that place. We enjoyed a new resolve, a new commitment to prayer, a new passion for each other, and a new hope for our work.

Our lives began to change as we drove away from that cabin, and nothing has ever been the same. The baby started sleeping at night, and our other problems suddenly became much more manageable. We struggled along the way, but the despair had lost its grip on us.

Over the next twelve years, we translated the Bible into that obscure West African language. We raised three kids in that village. Every anniversary, I would struggle to cultivate some blooming tree or bush in the rocky red gravel on the hill where our home stood just to make Rebecca smile. Today, a forest of flowers engulfs our former primitive, concrete-colored home—a monument that whispers of the love that blossomed in that place. I love my wife more every day, and I would never trade the life I have now for any other.

But to make our life of ministry work, we had to make a choice. To survive the challenge of the mundane, we had to choose prayer over despair. I believe God took me out on a limb and sawed it off because he wanted me to find out that he is real. I had always believed in him in the abstract, but now I knew him as an active participant in my life. He wanted me to learn that when it comes to success or failure, prayer is vital.

What do you do when your whole spiritual life seems to implode? Is God real to you, or do you rely on yourself? As you begin this book, you may find yourself distant from God in a parched spiritual wasteland. Your heart may no longer be stirred with any passion for him. Maybe you are troubled by unbelief because your past prayers seem to have gone unanswered. Well-meaning friends may have told you that the way to overcome your plague of doubts is just to

To survive the challenge of the mundane, choose prayer over despair.

pretend, to continue acting like you actually do believe. Eventually, they assure you, you will.

Pretending to have faith is not the way. You need to call to God to reveal himself to you in his power, and then wait for him to come and find you. "I waited patiently for the LORD; he turned to me and heard my cry. He lifted me out of the slimy pit. . . . He put a new song in my mouth, a hymn of praise to our God" (Psalm 40:1-3).

Effective prayer starts from a humble position of crying out to Jesus. Get on your knees in a quiet place and whisper, "God, I'm lost and I can't find you. I'll wait for you, but please come find me." Fall on your face and lift up the words of blind Bartimaeus, "Jesus, Son of David, have mercy on me!" (Mark 10:47). Try it again and again until you sense the distance closing between you and God. He meets us in our weaknesses and begins to move in power. The same Jesus who turned to meet Bartimaeus's need comes to us: "Go, your faith has healed you" (verse 52).

The eyes of the Lord roam the whole earth probing for people to strengthen,[1] not just spiritual giants but all those who choose to reach out to him in their darkest places. It's the trembling, outstretched arm that catches his attention—the undignified person begging for help whom he sees as bursting with potential, not only to be rescued, but also to strengthen others.

In fact, all good prayer begins from a position of weakness—not a lofty idea of our own spirituality. If we want our prayer life to be like climbing a ladder to heaven, that first rung needs to touch the mud in which we live. Once we choose prayer, God will lift us to the next step.

All good prayer begins from a position of weakness.

If you find yourself mired in ordinary struggles, you are not disqualified from practicing extreme prayer. That's actually an ideal place to start. Jesus prefers the cry of the person who says, "God, have mercy on me, a sinner" (Luke 18:13) over the pious smugness of those who have more faith in their own righteousness than in God.

I don't mean to say that once you start crying out to God from a point of desperation, you gradually become more confident and less dependent on God. No, desperation is pretty much the starting place for extreme prayer every time. The reason the Bible says God's mercies are new every morning [2] is that we need new mercy every day.

I hope we don't begin in a place of *despair* every time, but we need to pray from the posture of dependence that we learn from despair. Such reliance on God opens us up to the possibility of practicing extreme prayer. That's because the "extreme" in this type of prayer means trusting God to fulfill his promise to do "whatever we ask," to unleash his immeasurable glory in our families, communities, and ministries when we pray in the way Jesus prescribed.

When we call out to him with the impoverished spirit of a blind beggar, a sinful tax collector, or a prodigal child,

God always sweeps in to lift us up to a place we could never imagine. From our position as sons and daughters of the King, children of the Creator of the universe, we learn to ask without hesitation and without limit. That's how extreme prayer begins.

Questions for Reflection

1. Think of a time when you felt as if God had taken you out on a limb and then sawed it off. How did you grow spiritually in the process?

2. Describe a time when you felt spiritually dry and separated from God.

3. How do you think you ended up in a condition of spiritual dryness?

4. How have you overcome spiritually dry times in your prayer life?

5. Tell about a time when you were driven by your circumstances to pray more desperately than ever before? How were your prayers answered?

CHAPTER 1

BLANK CHECKS

Extreme Prayer Accesses the
"Whatever You Ask" Promises

AT THE START of our missionary career in West Africa, my wife and I moved into a dusty, tin-roofed shack in a small village, bringing only some basic supplies and two bicycles with us. We had visited the village with a more experienced colleague a few times before this to get to know the people; now we would live with the villagers as we began learning their language and culture.

Rather than house us in a grass-roofed hut, one of the church leaders sacrificially emptied his little square home for us. This house was like no dwelling we'd ever seen. I could reach up and touch the tin roof without stretching. The mice had burrowed through the floor and would pop up at night to eat anything not hanging from the ceiling. One night I heard a cataclysmic struggle in one corner. When I got up to investigate, I discovered a colossal spider wrestling a majestic roach. Rebecca and I cheered for the spider.

Outside, the drooping branches of a mango tree brushed up against the screenless window, providing convenient access into our home for green mamba snakes. Without a ceiling, our rafters were home to a host of bats roosting between the wood and the tin. Like some kind of bat cave, our little home had so many bat droppings on the floor that we could have supplied enough guano for the gunpowder used in the American Civil War.

In spite of our initial squeamish reaction, that house holds a special place in our hearts. The generous church leader who had allowed us to temporarily move into his home tried to help us adjust to the "openness" of our dwelling by explaining, "It's not only people who live in a house." His sacrificial loan enabled us to make our home among the people with whom we would work to translate the Bible into the Yalunka language.

When we first arrived in West Africa, we pulled our water out of a hand-dug well with a bucket. We cooked outside on a kerosene burner. I remember taking bucket showers out under the stars in a grass enclosure, thinking, *This is probably not what the Centers for Disease Control means when they caution Americans to avoid night-biting mosquitoes.* As I showered, I could look up to a night sky so stunningly bright that at first I mistook the Milky Way galaxy for a huge, wispy cloud stretching the width of the sky. One night about three months into our stay, I had an epiphany that I was gazing into a vast fog of distant stars.

A long, awestruck "oooh" flowed unbidden from my chest as I gaped at the same stars that had been God's visual aid for Abraham. I love Africa.

Living like the local people helped us get to know our neighbors. Just down the hill from us was a clearing where vendors set up a market every Saturday. Early our first morning, I heard trucks roaring to a halt outside. I tentatively opened the door to discover that our front steps were part of the market. Since our house was so close to the clearing, vendors were in the habit of stacking piles of rice just outside our doorway. Hundreds of people were milling around, hoping to catch a glimpse of the foreigners.

Another morning, the chilling wails of a mother in distress woke us. We found someone who could explain the woman's situation: her three-year-old son was dying. I felt so sad for this mother that I asked, "Could we see the child?"

I could tell by the villagers' faces that they had never considered that we might be able to help them. I wasn't a doctor. I had a good book on tropical medicine, but that was the extent of my medical training. Even I didn't know what I was thinking when I offered to help the dying boy.

They answered, "The child is out in the bush being treated by a traditional healer, but we will go out and get him."

It took a while for them to bring him back to the village, and I took advantage of the time to ponder my next move.

When Rebecca and I were finally brought to the boy, he was lying on the earthen floor of a grass-roofed hut belonging to one of his relatives in the village. His breathing was labored, and his pupils, wide like inky wells, did not respond at all to my flashlight. The words "pupils fixed and dilated," which I'd heard countless times on TV hospital dramas, echoed in my memory. Hopelessness crept into me as I realized that his mother was right; her son might not live long.

In hushed tones, Rebecca and I talked with the local pastor about what medical procedure might save the boy. "It can't be meningitis because we don't have any medicine for that," I mused, applying dubious diagnostics. "It could be cerebral malaria, but I don't know how to get an unconscious child to take the malaria tablets."

At some point I suggested, "We should pray for the kid. After all, we are missionaries."

At the simple mention of prayer, I saw the boy blink, and his eyes began to wander around the room focusing here and there.

I thought to myself, *We had better hurry up and pray, because I think God is healing him!* By the time we had finished praying, the boy's breathing was normal, and we were able to give him a dose of malaria medicine. Later that night, the family laughed festively over their little boy, whom they had given up for dead just hours before. We tried to give him the second dose of medicine that night, but he fought us like a rabid bobcat. His strength in combat proved to everyone present that he was fully recovered. Today he's nearly a grown man, and he still attends the village church.

In that dark hut a permanent little light blinked on inside my soul: *God is real, and he wants me to rely on him first, not as a last resort.* That's when I began to learn not to pray about my strategies, but to make prayer *the* strategy.[1]

> **I learned not to pray about my strategies, but to make prayer *the* strategy.**

I thought of that night twelve years later. My family was still living in that village, but by this time we had built a baked-brick home with solar power and a well with an electric pump that supplied running water. I was handed the receiver of our satellite telephone and heard the voice of the chairman of the board asking me to become the president of our mission, Pioneer Bible Translators.

When the euphoria of accepting this new challenge wore off, it occurred to me: *I'm in trouble. I need a really clever strategy.* Our ministry had a distinguished record in Bible translation; however, its growth had plateaued over the previous decade. As the new president of the mission, I couldn't show up without some kind of brilliant plan for success. People might figure out that I didn't know what I was doing! And the strategy had better be good, too, because if it didn't work, the failure of my leadership would be obvious to everyone.

Well, I *was* a Bible translator. So in desperation, I turned to the Bible and came across the "whatever" passages in the Gospels, the ones where Jesus says that when you pray a certain way he will give you "whatever you ask." I was stunned by Jesus' sweeping promises to answer our prayers, no matter how bold. Then I reflected on how God had answered so many prayers during our years serving in that village.

I thought, *Well, it sounds unsophisticated, but what if this prayer thing would really work? I'm supposed to believe the Bible; what if I tried doing what it says? How crazy is that?*

I decided to search Scripture[2] to discover the kinds of prayers that God has promised to answer and then to focus our whole mission on praying those prayers. That's as clever an approach as I could come up with. Prayer became our strategy. I thought, *What if we really could tap into the power of the reckless, blank-check promises Jesus makes?* What if you could too?

Prayer is a challenge for most of us. Some of us have never been taught what to do. Others are not convinced of the power of prayer. I consider myself a man of action, and prayer doesn't look like action. Many of us would rather work to get something done than pray. Leaders are especially activity oriented and typically not known as prayer warriors. We might be tempted to look at long prayer times as navel gazing. We can pray for a little while, but then we get antsy. We feel like we need to get out there and make things happen.

While at a convention recently, I heard a man announce over the loudspeaker, "We have just made a miracle happen here." Any miracle we can make is not from God. However, I believe I have finally learned something about how to access the promises of Jesus to answer *whatever I ask* in prayer. The power unleashed by this approach has made me want to pray longer and more often. I've come to see prayer as *the* work.

We get antsy after praying for a while. We feel like we need to get out and make things happen.

So when I returned to the United States to lead our mission, I came with the strategy of prayer. I knew that several Bible-less people groups had been asking our mission to translate the Bible for a decade, but we'd never had enough people. Thinking about that, I was filled with a sense of dissatisfaction. It just wasn't good enough for a Bible translation mission to leave people without Scripture for a decade while they continued to hunger for it.

I decided we needed to roughly double in size to meet the needs we already had identified in the countries we served, as well as to begin work in four new fields. I knew that our tiny, packed modular building would not support the goal of doubling in size. So I announced new goals that were big enough to make me nervous:

> We would double in size over the next six years.
> We would construct a permanent headquarters facility.
> We would start projects to meet all the translation needs in our current fields.
> We would start translation work in four more countries.

How would we do that?

> We would pray the kinds of prayers Jesus promised he would answer with unlimited power.

The strategy would have been pretty lame except for one detail: God is real. He's more real and powerful than any forest fire, hurricane, or tsunami. He will release his incomparable power into your ministry for the purpose of his Kingdom if you learn to pray the prayers he promised to answer.

Our ministry team decided to stake everything on God's power and on trusting him. We decided to become people of faith. God has overwhelmingly blessed that approach. His timing hasn't always matched ours exactly, but he has doubled the size of our mission. He has given us twenty-two acres and a building. We can see him working to meet the translation needs in our original fields. We have started work in seven more countries instead of four.

Now we know that no other strategy will be good enough for us. We are becoming a people of faith, gradually increasing our commitment to prayer as we see God moving in increasing power.

So what do I mean when I say *extreme prayer*? I mean intentionally praying the kinds of prayers that tap into all of Jesus' open-ended promises about prayer in a way that achieves maximum Kingdom impact.

I base the idea of extreme prayer on a study and application of the scriptural promises of Jesus to do whatever we ask when we pray certain ways. The idea of extreme prayer is that Jesus sprinkled "whatever you ask" passages throughout the New Testament to coax us into trying them out. When we begin to experiment with them, God will build our faith in him through his mighty answers to prayer. He will teach us how to come to know him by learning what he is passionate about and working alongside him to accomplish his mission.

> **Extreme prayer taps into Jesus' open-ended promises about prayer in a way that achieves maximum Kingdom impact.**

Extreme prayer is not the only way to pray; it's not a replacement for praying about your individual needs. I'm proposing an addition to the normal kinds of prayer that people usually pray. You may have learned the memory aid ACTS to help you remember how to pray. It's helpful to point out that your prayer times should start with adoration (*A*) and include confession (*C*). You should not forget thanksgiving (*T*). After covering those basics, you can go on to supplication (*S*) and make the kinds of requests Jesus modeled for your basic needs, such as "give us this day our daily bread." It's important to intercede for leaders in the world. It's crucial to pray for the sick people in your community. I'm not trying to replace all that. Rather I'm proposing you add an *E* on the end to include boldly praying the kinds of extreme prayers that Jesus commanded you and me to pray.

Since ACTSE doesn't spell anything, I think a better memory aid is to strive to have an ACTIVE prayer life.

Adoration—worshiping God for who he is

Confession—admitting and repenting of our sin

Thanksgiving—lifting up our gratitude for what God has done

Intercession/Supplication—praying for ourselves and others

Vanquishing Satan—practicing regular spiritual warfare

Extreme Prayer—maximizing all the prayer promises of Jesus

By the way, take note of the *V* for vanquishing Satan and his demons by practicing regular spiritual warfare. I learned this type of prayer in Africa, too, and Scripture explains why it is so critical. Revelation 12 teaches that demons were angels whom God kicked out of heaven after they rebelled against him. They are filled with bitter hatred, but since they can't harm God, they do the next best thing. They attack the people God loves, trying to wound him indirectly by hurting his children and persuading them to turn away from him.

If you're like most Americans, though, you have a hard time imagining that you are surrounded by unseen spiritual forces. You may believe that demons are real, but you may not think they impact you in any concrete way. That's similar to the response I got whenever I tried to explain bacteria to a Yalunka villager:

"This disease is caused by germs."

"Where are they?"

"They are too small to be seen."

"Well, how can they hurt me then?"

"There are millions of them. They are on every surface, and they can cause disease."

"Really?"

Even I could tell that I sounded like a lunatic. The Yalunka people would just shake their heads at the poor deluded Westerner.

And yet demons are very real to the people of West

Africa. In the area where Rebecca and I worked, people have been sacrificing chickens and sheep to demons for hundreds of years. I remember a time when the Yalunka church prayed for a man who was so full of demons that it took four people to hold him down. The demons left and he became sane again. Demons are a real but unseen power in the same way bacteria are real, powerful, and unseen.

Paul teaches us to fight against our unseen enemy. He says,

> Put on the full armor of God, so that you can take your stand against the devil's schemes. For our struggle is not against flesh and blood, but against the rulers, against the authorities, against the powers of this dark world and against the spiritual forces of evil in the heavenly realms. Therefore put on the full armor of God, so that when the day of evil comes, you may be able to stand your ground, and after you have done everything, to stand.
>
> EPHESIANS 6:11-13

The word translated "stand your ground" means to stand in front of these powers. Paul is telling us to stand up to demons, to "resist" them.

The Bible uses the same word two other times:

Resist the devil, and he will flee from you.

JAMES 4:7

Your enemy the devil prowls around like a roaring lion looking for someone to devour. Resist him, standing firm in the faith.

I PETER 5:8-9

The *V* reminds us to follow the example and command of Scripture to "resist" Satan and his demons. Follow the example of the Lord's Prayer, saying, "Lord, deliver us from evil: evil thoughts, evil people, evil accidental events, and evil spirits. Lord, post your angels around us and our house to keep out evil. God, we give up all evil in our lives." Praying for God's protection and verbally rebuking the evil one can help prevent temptations from leading into addictions, conflicts into bitter fights, and sickness into death.[3]

While the *V* of ACTIVE is important, this book is centered on *E*, or *extreme prayer*—the discipline of maximizing Jesus' promises about prayer. Each of the following chapters unveils a different kind of prayer that Jesus backs with a blank-check promise. But watch out! Don't read this book to get your own wishes out of prayer. God wants something so much bigger than that. He longs to draw you to his side and to show you his dreams for your life and the lives of the people around you. Do you have the courage to let him?

Questions for Reflection

1. Which of your prayers has God seemed to answer with miraculous power?

2. When you pray, how much adoration, confession, and thanksgiving do you find yourself practicing before asking for what you want?

3. Why is it important to practice all the different aspects of prayer?

4. Do you spend time in spiritual warfare as you pray? If so, explain.

5. What does it mean to you that Jesus promises to do *whatever you ask*?

CHAPTER 2

NAME POWER

God Answers Prayer in Jesus' Name

RED DUST COATED the hodgepodge of grass-thatched huts, tin-roofed shacks, and two-story run-down palaces of past colonial glory in the town near our village home. The local residents proudly proclaimed that the great Niger River of West Africa, which originated nearby, flowed first through their town before meandering through a number of other countries and into the sea. Every week or two I would drive twenty minutes to this urban center of about thirty thousand residents to buy bread, antibiotics, and gasoline—the basic ingredients of our African missionary life.

After working in the area for a few years, I was driving over the Niger River and into town one day when I noticed a café that had an unfamiliar name slapped over the entryway in peeling, bold letters. Then I saw a truck rumble by with that same word emblazoned across the back in a makeshift paint job.

I wonder if angels held their breath in anticipation as

I asked, "What does that word mean?" One of my local Christian friends told me, "It's the name of the tribe that lives here in town, on the other side of the Niger River from our tribe."

That's how the missionaries of today first discovered the language group right next to us. I later found out that in the 1940s missionaries had served throughout that area, but somehow the current missions movement had lost track of this ethnic group. Until the day I learned about them and began researching their story, these people were so unreached that their language name did not grace any of the mission databases. I could find no mention of their ethnic group anywhere on the Internet.

God, of course, already knew all about them. He must have been pondering these same people when he interrupted Abraham's life four thousand years before, saying, "*All peoples* on earth will be blessed through you" (Genesis 12:3).*

In the coming months, I learned a bit more about this ethnic group that made its home across the river, including the fact that there were no Christians among them. One day when I was back in this town, I stopped on the side of the road to buy bread. While I was standing on the sidewalk, the mayor engaged me in conversation. Putting one hand on my shoulder, he glanced around until he was sure no

---

* Here and following, italics in Scripture portions indicate emphasis added by the author.

one could hear. After all, he was a leader who believed the Qur'an, and I was a man of the Bible. Then in a low, sonorous voice, he began singing hymns in his own language that he could remember from his childhood. I noticed just the slightest sheen of tears covering his eyes as he confided in a hushed whisper in French, "When I was a boy, the missionary lady taught us these songs around her piano. If you ever want to bring a missionary here, just let me know."

I thought, *Piano? How did the missionary lady get a piano in one piece to this hot, dusty end of the earth fifty years ago?* A series of images flashed unbidden into my mind as I imagined packing and moving a piano to the upper reaches of the Niger River in the 1940s. Then I regained focus as I realized that Jesus was at work in this man's life. Jesus had been toiling faithfully among these people long before we "discovered" them. I later learned that the previous generation of missionaries had started a church there. Then the political winds blew them out of the country, and the fledgling pastor had quit the faith. Though there was one church in town, it was a church of a few people from a different ethnic group, and it catered to the traditional ethnic rivals of these people, making it unlikely to be accepted by them.

Rebecca and I couldn't do anything practical to reach out to that community—or at least that's what our level of faith told us back then—so we resolved to simply pray. I had no idea the power that God would unleash in answering this kind of prayer. Whenever groups of visitors came from the United States, we would drive to the Niger River to pray together for these people. We would gaze out over that territory and its bustling throng of people and quietly plead with God that they would come to follow Jesus. I knew of no Christians among them. The local language had no Scripture. I knew of no plan for any missionary to come. We just prayed for God to reveal himself in this place.

After we had been praying for about a year, a West African missionary sent out by a church in a nearby people group came to town to show the *JESUS* film in a related language. Within two years, the attendance in the town's little church went from the ten extended family members to 180 people. Something vibrant began to happen. The same missionary who'd brought the film started a Bible study with about twenty of the local leaders. We were encouraged, so we kept praying.

Not long after, I heard that a Korean missionary, after surveying three different countries, had chosen to build a huge boarding school outreach right outside of town. This mission also started sending missionaries to reach out to this people group. Now I was convinced that God was answering our prayers.

When the Korean missionaries came, they found great spiritual openness. One village gave them over half a square mile of land for the school. A delegation came from town to confront the village leaders—defending the religion of the Qur'an. They fussed at the village for receiving Christ followers saying, "Don't you realize these people want to make you Christians?"

At that, one defiant member of the village council stood up and proclaimed, "I *am* a Christian!"

When I drove out to see what God was doing in answer to our prayers, the men of the village gathered. The local teacher of the Qur'an led everyone in a rousing chant of "Hallelujah!"—a word they had picked up from the West African missionary as he showed the *JESUS* film. I have never seen any teacher of the Qur'an shout "Hallelujah" before or since.

Not long after, Pioneer Bible Translators sent a family to that unreached people group to translate the Scripture into the local language. Now curious groups of people from various villages in the region have begun to meet to consider Christ and the Scriptures that are being translated into their language. As we continue to pray, God is establishing his church in several villages.

For two thousand years this people group remained virtually unaffected by the gospel and largely unknown to the church at large. Then everything changed—not because we came up with a brilliant strategy but because we made prayer *the* strategy. After two millennia of spiritual isolation, missionaries from three continents suddenly arrived. How could that happen? Only God could do it. Jesus promised that God would move in power like this whenever we pray *in Jesus' name*. We had asked for something central to the beating heart of our Savior: "The Lord is not slow in keeping his promise. . . . He is patient with you, not wanting anyone to perish, but everyone to come to repentance" (2 Peter 3:9).

What is the significance of praying in Jesus' name? In the Bible, a person's name represents his or her nature. Praying *in Jesus' name* doesn't mean asking for a Ferrari and tacking on the magic words "in Jesus' name." It means presenting requests that resonate with Jesus' character, praying "for his name's sake" prayers that advance his plans for the earth—in other words, proclaiming Kingdom of God–oriented prayers.

Praying in Jesus' name means presenting requests that resonate with Jesus' character and advance his plans for the earth.

Jesus' name comes from the Hebrew root word meaning "to save." Praying *in Jesus' name* literally means praying about obeying Jesus' command to bring his salvation to each person and to the ends of the earth. Prayers in Jesus' name center on the desire to see people far from God coming to know, love, follow, and obey Jesus.

The Gospel of John records Jesus proclaiming five similar promises about praying in his name:

> I will do whatever you ask *in my name*, so that the Son may bring glory to the Father.
>
> JOHN 14:13

You may ask me for anything *in my name*, and
I will do it.

JOHN 14:14

If you remain in me and my words remain in you,
ask whatever you wish, and it will be given you.

JOHN 15:7

You did not choose me, but I chose you and
appointed you to go and bear fruit—fruit that
will last. Then the Father will give you whatever
you ask *in my name*.

JOHN 15:16

I tell you the truth, my Father will give you
whatever you ask *in my name*. Until now you
have not asked for anything in my name. Ask and
you will receive, and your joy will be complete.

JOHN 16:23-24

Any promise that Jesus repeated five times just before
he died must be vitally important. Not only that, but the
Gospel of John is characterized by its stunning economy
of words. For instance, the most powerful claims for
the divinity of Christ are achieved with the two simple
words "I am." But this point about prayer in Jesus' name
carries such weight, unlocks such vast power, and is so

counterintuitive that John records five instances when Jesus repeated it so we would not miss it.

And when we really ponder these words, we have to ask, *Anything? Really? Whatever we ask?* Did Jesus really say "whatever we wish"? Is the sky too much? Is the ocean too big? Would he hand us the moon? Those things are way too small; he longs for us to open the horizon of our prayers to the eternal. Only the Word of God and the souls of people last forever, so those are the two most precious things on the planet. Pray that God would use your life to connect the Word of God to the souls of people. That's what praying *in Jesus' name* means.

Since only the Word of God and people last forever, we should pray that God would use our lives to connect his Word to the souls of people.

In the apostle John's letters, which appear near the end of the New Testament, he elaborates on the concept of "in Jesus' name." He repeats the promise of unlimited "whatever we ask" power twice in as many verses, although he replaces the words "in Jesus' name" with the words "according to his will," which in this context seem to mean the same thing:

This is the confidence we have in approaching God: that if we ask anything *according to his will*, he hears us. And if we know that he hears us—*whatever we ask*—we know that we have what we asked of him.

I JOHN 5:14-15

Praying in Jesus' name, John tells us, means praying the will of God for the world around us.

Why does God want us to pray his will? What is the advantage of our telling him about his will? It's not for his benefit, but for ours. He uses prayer as a way for us to come to know him. By praying and watching how God responds, we discover the passion of God's heart and the power of his response. Prayers that God's Kingdom would fill the earth attract the full zeal of heaven.

Jesus says that as his followers learn the "master's business" (John 15:15) and remain fruitful (John 15:4, 7), the Father will give them whatever they ask in Jesus' name—in other words, for his sake. When we pray persistently in faith but see no results, it may indicate that we are off God's target, but when we pray and see him unleash power, we discover more about the passion of heaven.

Most prayer meetings illustrate a more significant way in which we may have missed it. Instead of praying deliberately for the accomplishment of the mission of Jesus in the world, we spend most of our time praying for the things we would like to happen in our lives—for healing, a car, or a job. There's nothing wrong with lifting up these needs to Jesus, but we may not access the full measure of his "whatever you ask" power when we pray only those kinds of prayers. Limiting our petitions in this way may also be one reason few people get excited about prayer. They miss the opportunity to access more of the unbelievable power of Jesus' fivefold promise to do whatever we ask if our prayers are strategic to his nature and will. Only then will we be able to watch God moving in greater power.

If prayers for the sick characterize the prayer meetings you're a part of, Jesus' words to his disciples might apply to you too: "Until now you have not asked for anything *in my name*. Ask and you will receive" (John 16:24). Jesus did not promise to answer just any prayer the way you want. He promised to answer certain kinds of prayers, including the ones that match his plans for the world.

The bad news is that you might not get that Ferrari or that dream home after all. Your aunt might not be healed of arthritis. You might not be comfortable for the rest of your life. In this fallen world, loved ones will eventually die in spite of your prayerful pleas. It's not that God doesn't care. He grieves along with us, just as he did at the tomb of Lazarus,[1] anguished at the state of this world and our lives. However, the time has not yet come to wipe away every tear from our eyes in this imperfect world.[2]

The good news is that Jesus promises to release the full force of heaven when his people focus their prayers on his plan to redeem the people of this world, something he is passionate about. This is the core truth about extreme prayer: praying for the mission of God brings power beyond measure.

I was first introduced to extreme prayer long before I lived in West Africa—I just didn't recognize it yet. When I was in college, I signed up to go to South Padre Island, off the coast of southern Texas, over spring break with a ministry I was involved in. Our goal was to tell partying students about Jesus. (Spending the week on the beach while serving God was appealing, though as I look back, I'm not sure spring break on the Gulf Coast is the ideal setting for students to meet Jesus!)

Once there and facing the spectacle of peers reveling in beer and wet T-shirt contests, my fellow students and I were seized by paralyzing fear. How could we possibly approach any of these students with the gospel without looking like complete jerks?

Praying for the mission of God brings power beyond measure.

When we gathered together on the first morning of the trip, the leaders announced that we would spend that first day fasting and praying, approaching no one with the good news of Jesus—not until we had prayed. They dismissed us into the environment to go forth and encounter Jesus.

As I walked away from the others, I realized I was dressed more for summer than spring. I shivered in the cold, windy morning to the point that I was too distracted to pray outside. Not only that, I didn't believe prayer actually did much—not really. I believed my efforts were primary and prayer simply undergirded my hard work. Because I was eager to get started doing the "real" work, I figured I'd find a place to pray where people were gathered. That way I might bump into someone for a divine appointment.

So I popped into a Kentucky Fried Chicken, where I sat down at a booth to pray, grateful to be sheltered from the freezing coastal winds. I took out my Bible to read, but I was soon distracted by the enticing aroma of fried chicken, rolls, and french fries. My fast was less than an hour old, so I resisted the temptation—even though I was showing signs of crumbling resolve. I couldn't help but ask myself, *What kind of idiot fasts in KFC?*

Soon the place was bursting with hungry college students. After filling the booth across from me, a large, noisy group asked to overflow into my booth. My plan was working!

A mountain of a man scooted in next to me, taking up the majority of the booth. As he introduced himself, he told me he played center for a college football team in the Midwest. When he saw I had nothing to eat, he kindly bounced a biscuit filled with juicy chicken in front of me like a fumbled football. I sheepishly refused, "No, thank you. I'm fasting."

His eyebrows scrunched together as he focused on me in disbelief. "You're fasting in Kentucky Fried Chicken?"

he asked with more than a hint of skepticism. I didn't know what to say. Then, after a minute of thoughtful munching, he asked, "Have you ever wondered if it all might turn out not to be true?"

We sat and talked a long while, the fanatic and the football player. Eventually he introduced me to his friends. I don't know what they had been doing the previous night, but they appeared shaken by their out-of-control behavior. They agreed that one of their friends in particular urgently needed spiritual counsel after the previous night's partying.

They seemed to think it would be wise to have a conscience at the next bash, and they elected me. "Why don't you come tonight?" my new friends asked. I spent that night fidgeting in the kitchen at party central as one person at a time came to ask his or her spiritual questions.

When I showed up at the beach, I had been clueless, and my nerdy approach could never have generated the results I experienced. Yet that week actually worked out like a scene from the Gospels. I ended up surrounded by people in deep spiritual need. I got to testify and meet needs just like Jesus did. Looking back, I realize that the opportunity arose in the middle of fasting and prayer. In fact, I can't help but think that the only great and lasting results of my ministry have come out of prayer. Nothing seems to matter except what we choose to pray.

Look around your neighborhood, your church, and

the world. What is Jesus longing to do through you? Is it impossible? Perfect. Do you lack the resources to do it? Of course! Does it require knowledge and skills that you don't have? It usually does. Does it necessitate manpower you know you could never get? Most likely. Now try getting down on your knees and put the power switch in the "on" position.

When we made the impossible request that God would cause an obscure people in West Africa to come to know Jesus, he released the full measure of his glory. After all, he'd been talking about reaching all people since the time of Abraham. He was just waiting for us to ask. Jesus said that anyone who believes in him has access to his miraculous power: "I tell you the truth, anyone who has faith in me will do what I have been doing. He will do even greater things than these" (John 14:12).

Are you doing what Jesus did? Wouldn't you like to? You could be doing even greater things than Jesus himself! How is that possible? "Because I am going to the Father. And I will do *whatever you ask in my name*, so that the Son may bring glory to the Father. You may ask me for *anything in my name*, and I will do it" (John 14:12-14). Jesus promised to answer our extreme prayers about his plan of salvation with extreme power.

If you have faith in Jesus, start doing what he has been doing. Begin by asking him for marching orders every morning. Look around and ask yourself, *What would*

Jesus do in my community and workplace? What did Jesus command me to do in this world? What opportunities do I see before me that only fear prevents me from taking? What would I do if I only had faith and no fear?

Jesus said you will do even greater things than he if you pray in his name. Rather than sweating and pounding away in your own strength for precious few results, you need to get down on your knees and get some real work done. God answers prayers *in Jesus' name.*

Questions for Reflection

1. What does *in Jesus' name* mean?

2. How can your church or ministry pray *in Jesus' name?*

3. What has Jesus commanded in the Bible that your church or ministry should do in your community or the world?

4. Spend time praying for God to reveal his will for you and your workplace, ministry, or church. What do you think he desires for you to do as a result of those revelations?

5. What unattainable resources do you need in order to do Jesus' will in your community or the world? What insurmountable obstacles stand in the way?

6. Make a list of prayer requests designed to help you and your ministry overcome those obstacles and obey Jesus' commands more fully.

CHAPTER 3

BLIND TRUST

God Answers Prayers of Faith and Faithfulness

IN THE AFRICAN village where we lived, I regularly drove between the huts on a two-rutted track we had worn through the weeds. Beside that path leading to our home often sat an old man who had been blinded by cataracts. I drove right next to the stool he sat on almost every day and reflexively waved at him, though he never waved back.

One day I stopped to greet him. I spoke in the traditional terms of respect for an elderly man: "Father, whenever I drive by, I wave at you, but you can't see me, so you don't wave back." The man's face took on a sober look. In West Africa, it's a grave insult to refuse a greeting.

I said, "Let's try something new. Whenever you hear my car passing by, wave because you know I'm waving at you."

An enormous smile burst across the man's face. From that moment, every time I passed in my car, he and I would wave at each other. You know you have become a part of a community when even the blind man waves at you. He and I both enjoyed the secret bond we shared. I'll never forget the sly grin on his face every time he waved. For just a minute, it was as if he could see.

But what if the blind man hadn't waved when I drove by? I would have asked him, "Hey, didn't you believe me when I said I would wave to you?" If he treated me like I treat God sometimes, he would say, "Oh, sure I do. I believe you. Just because I don't act on my belief doesn't mean I don't believe." I would not be impressed by that. It's only because the man did wave at me even though he couldn't see me that I knew he really had faith in my word.

Like the blind man, we show our faith in God through our actions, even though we can't see him. Intellectual assent alone is not enough. In the Bible, faith without works isn't only dead, it's not even faith. There is no such thing as abstract faith apart from obedience.[1] The Hebrew root word from which we get the biblical idea of faith means to consider something to be solid even though it's unseen.[2] The degree of faith we have is shown by the degree to which we are faithful. We prove our faith by our actions.

By now, I've seen too many answers to prayer to really doubt the existence of God, but I am skeptical about the existence of my faith at times. If biblical faith implies beliefs backed up by actions, then that helps us understand what Jesus teaches about prayer when he says,

Have faith in God. . . . I tell you the truth,
if anyone says to this mountain, "Go, throw
yourself into the sea," and does not doubt in his
heart but believes that what he says will happen,
it will be done for him. Therefore I tell you,
whatever you ask for in prayer, believe that you
have received it, and it will be yours.

MARK 11:22-24

In Matthew, Jesus finishes this same lesson with the sweeping statement, "If you believe, you will receive *whatever you ask for* in prayer" (Matthew 21:22). When Jesus says, "Have faith in God" (Mark 11:22), his words also challenge us to live out our faith. (The same Greek word is translated as both "believe" and "have faith" in the New Testament.) We all struggle between believing and lacking faith. Jesus throws down the faith gauntlet for everyone stuck between the seen and unseen worlds, between sight and faith. He staunchly challenges us all, saying, "Everything is possible for him who believes" (Mark 9:23).

I've tossed the Greek in that Scripture like a salad, and it simply means what it says. If we have faith in God and live out that faith, the extreme answers to prayer we may see are limitless.

Does this passage work like magic? It seems to imply that if you close your eyes and repeat something enough, it will happen. That's not quite it. Jesus can't be talking about an I-do-believe-in-fairies approach to life, making a wish and getting it every time. The whole conditional key to this principle is that we must live out true faith in God, submitted to his lordship and his will for this earth. We cannot manipulate our Lord with prayer as if it were magic.

He's talking about the kind of lifestyle we find in Hebrews 11 describing people of faith:

By faith these people overthrew kingdoms,
ruled with justice, and received what God had
promised them. They shut the mouths of lions,
quenched the flames of fire, and escaped death by
the edge of the sword. Their weakness was turned
to strength. They became strong in battle and
put whole armies to flight. Women received their
loved ones back again from death.
    But others were tortured, refusing to turn
from God in order to be set free. They placed
their hope in a better life after the resurrection.
Some were jeered at, and their backs were cut
open with whips. Others were chained in prisons.
Some died by stoning, some were sawed in half,
and others were killed with the sword. Some went
about wearing skins of sheep and goats, destitute
and oppressed and mistreated. They were too
good for this world.

HEBREWS 11:33-38, NLT

Jesus promises to answer prayers of faith, which also implies faithfulness. John uncovers the connection between belief, faith, and faithfulness too:

> Dear friends, if our hearts do not condemn us, we have confidence before God and receive from him *anything we ask*, because we *obey his commands* and do what pleases him. And this is his command: *to believe* in the name of his Son, Jesus Christ, and to love one another as he commanded us.
>
> I JOHN 3:21-23

John says we receive anything we ask only when we obey God's commands and do what pleases him. The command is to believe, and when we believe, we obey Christ's commands. Belief and obedience are bound tightly in an inseparable unity as prerequisites for getting whatever we ask. We must believe and obey to see power in prayer.

James says, "The prayer offered in faith will make the sick person well. . . . The prayer of a righteous man is powerful and effective" (James 5:15-16). By definition, the prayer of faith is offered by a righteous person who lives out his or her faith. Faith becomes faithfulness when people obey God because of their faith in him.

Doubt, Jesus says, is the enemy of faith-filled prayer: "I tell you the truth, you can say to this mountain, 'May you be lifted up and thrown in the sea,' and it will happen. But you must really believe it will happen and have no doubt in your heart" (Mark 11:23, NLT).

James uses the same Greek word: "But when he asks, he must believe and not doubt" (James 1:6). The word *doubt* in Greek is related to a word that means "judge" or "discern." Does our prayer life show

Belief and obedience are prerequisites for getting whatever we ask and for seeing power in prayer.

that we believe God, or are we applying our cynical judgment to him by telling ourselves, *If God answers this prayer the way I want, then I will believe he is a good God*? That's one form of doubt in the Bible: evaluating God's actions based on how well he does what we want. But *he* is not subject to our inspection and approval. Instead, we must pray with faith and faithfulness, submitting ourselves to God.

So when God decides not to answer such a prayer, does that mean we have no faith? We must not jump to this conclusion either. When I was in college, I attended a Sunday school class called "Signs and Wonders." Our teacher, David, who was confined to a wheelchair, demonstrated maturity and spirituality in everything he did and said.

Each Sunday we would watch a video presentation on how supernatural events orchestrated by the Holy Spirit, such as prophecy and healing, could draw unbelievers to Christ. After the video concluded, we'd completely disregard the biblical teaching, and amateur hour would begin. Every Sunday one of the men in the class—let's call him Jim—would get up. With a dramatic, faraway look in his eyes, he'd put one hand on our teacher's shoulder.

"David, this is the Sunday you will finally have the faith. Today you will finally rise up out of that chair by faith in Jesus! Let's all pray for David to believe and reclaim his legs." My gut always clenched up as we put enormous pressure on David, thoroughly blaming his paralysis on his lack of faith. We all went along with it, Sunday after Sunday, but I felt like making a whip of three cords and driving Jim out of the class.

We must pray with faith and faithfulness, submitting ourselves to God.

What unbelievable courage this paralyzed man exhibited. I was so impressed with his poise. There was something wrong with Jim's theology, but I couldn't put my finger on it biblically. In Jim's interpretation, David's infirmity became an occasion to judge him as faithless. I don't know why David wasn't healed in spite of his obvious faith. I don't fully understand that part of God's Word in this situation.

After many weeks, David finally dealt with Jim in his own way. Getting an uncharacteristic faraway look, he said, "Jim, today is the day that we are going to pray for financial healing for you and your family. We know that you are suffering in financial bondage right now. We are going to form a circle around you and march around you seven times, praying aloud. After the seventh time, the financial walls of Jericho will collapse around you, and you will be healed."

I thought it was a swell idea. Immediately we all rose and formed a phalanx around our brother Jim, orbiting him like noisy prayer satellites. We eagerly prayed aloud for Jim's financial healing to the exclusion of all other thought, and things went along splendidly until we each individually began to realize that no one was keeping count. First one and then more of us began to glance at one another for cues about when to stop circling Jim. It seemed somehow unholy to be the first to suggest we knock it off. At some point the satellite effect gradually looked more like a flock of confused buzzards circling, hesitantly looking around and praying distractedly. David, for some reason, never did tell us to quit. Eventually we just stopped and flopped down in our chairs one at a time. I always wondered if Jim received financial freedom, but I will never know. As I recall, he never returned to the class.

Did David's paralysis really have its roots in his lack of faith? Would Jim have received financial healing if we had added one more orbit around him? Somehow I don't believe that. The Bible teaches us that God works powerfully through weak earthen vessels to more perfectly manifest his own power.[3] Jesus said that one man was born blind "so that the work of God might be displayed in his life."[4] None of us like to be weak and suffering, but when we accomplish something in spite of our inevitable frailty,

God's glory is magnified, and we get a more accurate picture of our own tender need for him.

God desires that we know him and love him as he really is, and we need to learn to long for our spiritual home with him in heaven. We learn through weakness that this world is not our home, that the current creation is twisted by human sin, and that God will replace it with a perfect one.[5] He will not answer prayer in a way that might distort our perception of his nature or the fallen state of this world. Some of our prayers go unanswered because they are not consistent with the nature of God. Sometimes God's reasons exceed our human capacity to grasp, and we just have to apply the principle of the faith-filled complaint that we'll explore in chapter 7.

> **When we accomplish something in spite of our frailty, God's glory is magnified, and we get a more accurate picture of our need for him.**

We all know from experience that we never receive some things we pray for, even though we think we are praying in faith with great perseverance. Just because our prayers are not answered as we expect does not necessarily mean our faith is the problem. We find ourselves in a fallen world, with all of creation groaning with imperfection.

Did David really doubt God as we prayed? If he did, I couldn't see it. He just sat there as steady as a brick, working to teach the Bible to the people around him. God just was not ready to deviate from the natural plan of this fallen world—not then anyway. In my mind, it was no reflection on David. In fact, if Jesus doesn't return first, I'm sure one day David will die, no matter how much we pray for him or how much faith he has. It would be shortsighted to impugn David's faith because he died as a part of the natural pattern of this world.

After all, David, Jim, and the rest of us are headed toward the same door in this world, and we all must suffer along the way. Jesus himself promised that in this world we will have trouble.[6] It is the nature of this place. We are not told why some prayers are answered and some are not. Any effort to evaluate whether God has answered all our prayers before Christ comes again is premature. God will finish answering some of them after Jesus returns.

We *are* told, however, that God invites us to pray in faith and faithfulness, and he promises great power to those who do. We must not doubt by discerning or evaluating God's goodness based on his answer to prayer. We simply pray in faith, living the most faith-filled lives we know how. Then we watch and wait for God's provision. Jesus teaches that God answers prayers when our life choices radiate from our faith. Grow in faith, and the power of your prayer life will grow along with it. Pray, and God's answers will grow your faith.

One moonless night in West Africa, I awoke to a voice calling at the window in that desperate tone that marks middle-of-the-night emergencies—hushed yet urgent enough to rouse me. My friends in the village had come to rely on me for medical help at any hour of the night, so none of this struck me as unusual. Often I would drive people to the hospital. But this night was not like that.

As I rolled out of bed, I heard my neighbor at the window say, "Aisha is breathing again, but come quick." As I dressed, I turned that phrase over in my mind. I didn't even know that Aisha was sick. When I stumbled my way down the hill and entered her hut, I found Aisha peacefully sleeping, surrounded by wide-eyed church members.

The leader of the women in the church said, "She quit breathing and her arms got cold. Then we prayed for her. She started breathing again and her arms warmed back up."

I stared at them for a minute processing that worldview bombshell. What could I say, "Keep up the good work"? All I could do was add my prayers to theirs and stumble back to bed. To this day I have no idea what tropical disease nearly killed Aisha.

Who among us has the faith to pray for a woman when she's growing cold, already brushing against the threshold of death's door? These faithful believers did. God answers prayers of faith and faithfulness.

Questions for Reflection

1. Faith does not exist apart from obedient action. What does that tell us about the need to act on

our beliefs and the importance of obedience in our Christian walk?

2. What actions in your life prove that your faith exists?

3. What do you do in your church, ministry, or workplace that would be impossible without God's power and that benefits only him?

4. Have you ever felt like you prayed in faith, but you didn't get what you prayed for? Why do you think that happened?

5. Describe the type of prayers we pray that reveal a lack of faith in God.

6. Describe a time when you prayed for something even though you felt your faith was weak. How did God answer your prayer?

7. Develop a plan to grow your faith. How can you start implementing the plan in practical ways during the coming week?

WHEN YOU WERE a kid, did you ever dream of getting something with an almost religious fervor? Maybe you were absolutely dying to own a puppy or a Nintendo or a pool like the kid's next door. I don't know why I didn't just ask my mother for the sword I wanted; I just remember yearning for a little plastic sword in the worst way when I was about four years old.

My mother had taught me about prayer, so I began to ask God for that sword. I prayed regularly for what seemed like months to my four-year-old mind. Persistent prayer was no small feat for a boy with a fifteen-second attention span. Though there was no sign of God answering, I kept hard after him. I remember the conversations in the dark of my room as I was drifting off to sleep. "God, pretty please with sugar on top, if only I could have a sword."

Back then my view of God was small. I turned to him when the darkness in the room made me tremble in terror.

I didn't know if he listened, but I was pretty sure he lingered in one upper corner of my bedroom ceiling.

My answer came one day when my family visited the beach. We were packing up and getting in the car when I ran back for one last gallop by the waves. There, half thrust into a crumbling sand castle, appeared a silver plastic sword. I looked around and saw nothing but deserted beach, no possible owner nearby. The theme music from *The Lord of the Rings* should have been playing in the background as I reached to pluck the sword from the sand.

I would think back on this moment for more than a few decades: it was the first instant I knew for sure that God was not confined to that corner of my room and that he listened to the longings of my unsatisfied soul. I can still remember the reassuring texture of the bumpy design on the sword's grip and the awkward angle of the blade, a scar from some forgotten battle. I can remember the way it smelled and the feel of its frayed edges, a testimony to overzealous hacking during some monumental conflict.

When my mother saw how much I loved that sword, she bought newer, better-quality ones, but the beach castoff is the one etched in my earliest memories. That formidable weapon in my hand came to be a tangible sign of the simple truth: God answers persistent prayer.

Jesus has been teaching this lesson for two thousand years. When the disciples asked, "Lord, teach us to pray,"

Jesus told a story about an insistent friend. Later, he reinforced the point with a story about a persistent widow.[1] He tells both stories "to show them that they should always pray and not give up" (Luke 18:1).

In one story, a needy widow begs for justice from a corrupt judge, who resists her request. Because she pleads with him over and over, though, he finally concludes, *This lady is unbelievable! She just won't quit. I had better give her what she wants or she will wear me out!* Shameless persistence pays off. After telling this story, Jesus encourages us to "cry out to him day and night," promising to answer "quickly" (Luke 18:7-8).

Shameless persistence pays off.

Jesus also paints a picture of an audacious man who pounds on his neighbor's door, asking to borrow food in the middle of the night (Luke 11:5-13). Can you imagine yourself being that pushy at midnight in your neighborhood? The porch light blinks on. In his pajamas, your neighbor squints out the peephole. He's fumbling with a shotgun and a few shells when he suddenly recognizes you. *Oh, it's that crazy neighbor.*

After he stops his wife from dialing 911, he gives you some food just to get rid of you. "The nerve of that guy!" he grumbles as he shuffles back to bed.

One English translation tries to make the man's request sound noble by calling it "boldness" (Luke 11:8). The word in Greek means "shameless" or "impudent." The night-calling neighbor has no sense of what is proper. He's beyond caring about social niceties. He's going to pound on that door until somebody comes and meets his need, no matter how rude and improper he seems. When Jesus finishes sketching this odd scene, he casts you and me in the eccentric role in the play. He challenges us to pray "shamelessly," to pound rudely on the door of heaven with boundless audacity at all hours and beyond all sense of propriety. "Ask and it will be given to you; seek and you will find; knock and the door will be opened to you" (Luke 11:9).

I've seen this kind of persistence before. One day two blind men from my West African village came to my porch. "Sir, we are completely entrusting ourselves to you," they announced. "We have complete confidence that you will help us to see again." Never mind the fact that I didn't know anything about eyes or medicine.

We missionaries are not without our resources, however. I made a good speech about God's power, and I prayed for the two men. I rummaged around in my medicine cabinet and pulled out worm medicine and vitamins, which I gave them. I've seen that combination cure almost anything.[2]

Over generations, the people of this part of western Africa have developed immune systems that Americans could never dream of possessing. Malaria and several types of disease-causing organisms are part of their normal baseline health. It's generally not until they get a fourth or fifth illness that they seek medical attention. Often if you can eradicate one or two of their illnesses, their immune systems can crush the remaining invading organisms like beetles on a highway.

So I developed a reputation as a miracle worker by giving out worm medicine and vitamins. People sometimes walked all day long—even from another country—to get to my front porch. (If you came to my porch today in Texas, I'd be tempted to offer you worm medicine and vitamins as a knee-jerk reaction.)

After those two blind men left, I thought that was the last of it. But like human boomerangs, they came back almost every day. What else did two blind men have to do with their time? On their first visit, an adult held their hands and guided them to my door. The next time, a kid led them to my door. But once their fellow villagers realized that these men would continue to visit me every day, no one was willing to bring them, not even the kids. So they would stumble through the village, searching for my home.

One of them could just barely make out subtle shades of color, so he would lead the other in search of my door. When I watched them meandering about the town, I thought of Jesus' parable about blind guides. I am not proud of it, but more than once as they were getting close to our home, I got really quiet so they couldn't find us. *Shh, it's the blind men. Nobody make a sound!* I would hiss at my kids.

Don't judge me! Whenever they would find me, I would sit with them on the porch for an hour or sometimes much longer, sometimes praying, sometimes giving them a little medicine, always investing a big chunk of my day because I believed Jesus would want it that way. I tried to remain compassionate, but their daily visits absolutely wore me out. On top of that, deep down I had stopped believing my prayers were doing any good. Yet these men were the very image of dogged, unashamed perseverance.

After a while, though, they stopped coming. One day as I walked in the village, I saw one of the men's relatives and asked what had happened to them. I almost fell over when he told me that one of the men had received his sight.

Now why was I, a prayerful missionary, so surprised by that? The teaching of Jesus is true: God answers persistent prayer. In this instance, I don't understand why he didn't answer the persistent prayers of the other blind man too. I can't explain why I haven't seen answers to all of my prayers either. But I have learned that the prayers God chooses to answer are most often persistent ones.

I don't know about you, but I don't like the theological picture Jesus paints with the parables of the pesky neighbor and the tenacious widow. Is God really comparing himself to a corrupt judge or a neighbor who's slow to answer the door at night? Actually, I don't think Jesus was trying to draw a perfect parallel between God and these questionable characters. Nor was he suggesting that God gives us what we want because he is sick of us or just wants us to go away. The point is not that God is like the judge; it's that we need to learn to be more like the widow. And while God doesn't sleep in a bed at night, we still need to learn to knock like the neighbor.

We might prefer to pray to a God of convenience, but Jesus is teaching us something else about our heavenly Father: he responds to those who persevere in prayer. God's insistence that we rely on repeated prayer is not about him, but about us learning that he is the source of power. If not for having to pray persistently, wouldn't we take credit for God's powerful miracles and completely ruin ourselves with arrogance? Our pride would lead to the swelling of our heads and the suffocation of our souls.

Tenacious prayer builds faith and minimizes pride. If God had healed the two blind men after their first visit, I would have thought, *Wow, that worm medicine and vitamin treatment is even better than I thought.* But when God healed one of them only after we'd prayed together for months, we knew beyond all doubt what had happened. God was at work.

Tenacious prayer builds faith and minimizes pride.

In fact, before this I had assumed that maybe the worm medicine *did* work wonders. For example, one day when I was walking in a distant village, a lady came up to me and said, "Do you remember me? I was blind and came to your house once. You gave me medicine, and now I can see." While I'm sure I prayed for her after giving her the medication, I thought, *Hey, I need to know what miraculous medicine I gave her.*

So I said, "The pills I gave you—what did they look like?" She immediately turned to ask the people around her, "Remember that medicine he gave me? What did it look like?"

I thought, *Wow, she really was blind.* (I can just imagine the scene in heaven when missionary bloopers are replayed on the eternal JumboTron. When they get to this scene, Jesus will wryly comment, "My favorite part is where Greg asks the blind lady, 'What did those pills look like?'")

Did I really think that worm medicine and vitamins alone would heal the blind? How frustrating was that for God? Why did I not get the message until the two blind men? Because that's when God waited to act until I'd prayed persistently with them.

You and your church or ministry may be in a similar situation right now. For example, if you make a great plan to reach your city with the gospel but fail to pray doggedly about it, the only compassionate thing for God to do is doom your plan to failure so you won't swell with pride. Attributing a successful campaign to great leadership or dynamic worship is the equivalent of putting your faith in vitamins and worm medicine.

Out of mercy God may not grant you and me success in our ministry until we persist in prayer. He may withhold his power until an entire community is united in prayer, making the same request over and over. That way, when he acts, we won't be tempted to give credit to some earthly person or strategy.

Instead, we will think of all those rug burns on our knees, fall on our faces in reverent awe, and give glory to the Creator of the universe, who hears our cry and moves in power at the point of our weakness. This is how God wants our ministry to work. He wants to build our faith in him—not in any program or personality. Then he can more freely release his power into our lives.

Jesus finishes the parable of the widow with what I think is the saddest lament in the Bible: "When the Son of Man comes, will he find faith on the earth?" (Luke 18:8). The grief in his voice becomes more troubling when the full impact of the original language is rendered: "When I come back, I won't find faith on the earth, will I?" You can hear the heartrending pain of God's disappointment with our hard hearts. I would paraphrase it this way: "I guess it's really too much to expect that these spiritually frail human beings will believe in me."

I yearn with all my heart to astonish Jesus with my faith; to make absolutely sure that when he returns, he will find faith in me and in you. But I have to admit that my faith sometimes appears bankrupt even in my own eyes. It's harder to sustain than I'd like to admit.

Persevering in prayer has been the greatest way I have

found to build faith in my diseased heart. In fact, I challenge you to stop reading for a minute, get down on your knees, and pray with me, "Jesus, you will find faith on the earth. You will find it in us." God himself will create faith in our hearts by answering determined prayer.

The bad news is that God usually won't move in power without considerable prayer. The good news is that persistence pays off. There is nothing complicated about praying over and over again. We can all do that! Jesus promises to answer when we do.

Questions for Reflection

1. Describe a time when you have given someone something just because that person would not quit asking.

2. What aspect of that experience is like the way God answers our prayer? How is God much higher and purer in his answers to prayer?

3. Describe a time when you became angry with God for not answering your prayer. What impact did that have on your faith?

4. Describe a time when your prayer was answered and you took partial or all the credit for it. How did that impact your faith?

5. Think about a time when you prayed for something for a long time and finally got it. How did that impact your faith?

6. Why do you think God expects us to pray repeatedly for things?

7. What do you intend to begin praying for consistently this week? Consider making a prayer list for your church or ministry so you can begin persevering in prayer for those requests.

CHAPTER 5

THE SYMPHONY

God Answers Unified Group Prayer

WHEN GOD CALLED me to lead our mission, we moved from the bush of Africa to the suburbs of Dallas. That was an adjustment! There was a time in Africa when I would walk out my door with my rifle slung over my shoulder, looking to shoot any nearby animal for meat. Now, my neighbors don't like that. My yard in Africa had elephant grass eight feet tall, so excuse me if I don't think four-inch-high Bermuda grass is a state of emergency. My lawn care in Africa was limited to the judicious use of a sharp machete, so don't expect me to know much about proper edging.

Our kids had a hard time adjusting too. At the time of our move, Hannah was eleven, Abigail was nine, and Paul was seven. Someone asked one of girls, "When you were in Africa, did you eat anything exotic?"

She thought for a minute and said, "Well, do you consider warthog exotic?"

We had to let her know that, yes, for future reference, baboon kabobs, monkey, Cape buffalo, duiker, honey bee larva, termites, and python eggs are all classified by some folks as exotic.

One day my daughter was looking at the school calendar when she turned to me with a look of shock. "Dad," she gasped, "what is Spirit Day?" I knew what she was thinking, so I tried to help her out. "Well, sweetie, that's when they sacrifice a goat to the ancestors."

She soberly took the bait. "Dad, they shouldn't have that on the school calendar."

When in kindergarten, my other daughter hesitated to go with the teacher to the "restroom" because she wasn't sleepy. One of the kids came home wanting to know, "What is a mall, and why is it so special?"

I remember the day my kids saw us mailing a letter for the first time. "Oh," my daughter commented, "I thought that was pretend." She hadn't realized that there really was a postal service and that a letter carrier really did come to our house every day just to pick up my personal messages, which would be delivered around the world.

It's hard to move from one culture to another. You never get it all figured out. We have never fully adjusted from the years spent living in the bush. When I took my kids to the Fort Worth Zoo, its warthog exhibit made me so hungry! To the horror of the people around us, my kids passed the zoo's exhibits pointing out all the species we had eaten. "Oh look, Dad, a pangolin—just like that time . . ."

Coming home was an adjustment for everyone in the family, but the real fine-tuning came when I had to figure out how to lead a ministry. When you lead, rumor has it, you are supposed to set goals. Our team had set the goal of more than doubling the number of teammates over a six-year period. I know I sounded crazy the day I announced to our mission's board, "Ladies and gentlemen, we have an ambitious goal to double in size over the next six years." My eager and supportive board leaned in to hear my detailed planning: "Ahem, well, in order to achieve the goal, we plan to pray a lot."

I'm sure it seemed pretty basic. I mean, weren't we praying a lot before this time anyway? We were missionaries after all. Even so, the best strategy I could muster was to intentionally pray the kinds of prayers Jesus promised to answer. I figured that if our commitment to prayer gradually increased over time, and if those prayers conformed to Jesus' promises, we would attract the full focus and power of heaven. I imagined the eyes of the Lord roaming the earth, seeking a group of people to use powerfully in his Kingdom. I wanted him to pause and say, "Hey, look at these people; they are trusting me more each day."

We started adding prayer events and corporate times of fasting to our calendar. We worked to fill in a 24/7 prayer schedule with all the missionaries around the world. We wanted to continually ramp up prayer over time to keep attracting God's favor and blessing.

Of course, we also made choices consistent with our prayers, worked really hard, and tried to stay alert for how God was moving around us to answer our prayers. Even so, normally leaders can't just say, "Hey, let's double in size," and have that work out. They need more action than that. Good leaders know you need to pour resources into a plan for it to work.

As resources go, prayer outperformed anything I've ever seen. I calculated that we would need to transition gradually, growing at a higher annual rate each year. I had lined out target personnel numbers to help us determine whether we were on track. When you plan to initiate an exponential growth curve, the first three years out of six are the easy ones. The last three are where the miracle really becomes apparent. By year four, in 2010, we smacked into a speed bump. We needed to accelerate our growth a lot that year, but by the end of May we had only ten new recruits and around twelve more possible candidates. We were starting to feel disappointment as we faced the facts: there was no possible way to end the year with our goal of forty-five new teammates. We could see we were on track to get only half the new recruits we needed that year.

These weren't just numbers either; these numeric goals represented new missionaries needed to translate Scripture for Bible-less people to bring God's transforming power to whole cultures that lacked Scripture. We knew Jesus had an interest in what we were doing, but where were all the new missionaries for whom we had been praying?

As Christians sometimes do when their faith is challenged, we began to rationalize all the reasons God had not answered. Maybe our team just couldn't handle that kind of growth.

As resources go, prayer outperformed anything I've ever seen.

Things had been pretty hectic lately after all. God, in his mercy, had given us a lull in the increase. Maybe this was a time to consolidate our gains and finally get organized and write some job descriptions. Abandoning the goal as just a bit unrealistic began to sound rational. After all, how many Americans really wanted to leave their comfortable homes to move to some of the most politically unstable malarial zones on the planet? Of course it wasn't working out!

Yet before abandoning the goal entirely, we declared a fast for May 26 and 27. We prayed one more time for God to bring us the right missionaries. It was just two days of mild hunger, but something about that time must have changed the way God saw the situation. It didn't feel any different. I finished fasting and hit the Chinese buffet without hearing any thunderous voices from above. But while we were going back to business as usual, somewhere in heaven, a floodgate of grace opened.

Have you ever been stampeded at a summer camp

when the dinner bell rings? New missionaries herded into our mission like hungry campers at a cafeteria. By the end of the year we blew right by the goal of forty-five new recruits. There was no natural, rational explanation for it. One month we had a few people; the next, we had a crowd. Forget writing job descriptions and getting organized, we were pulling out all the stops just to incorporate growth! If I had been an atheist witnessing that moment, it would have been enough to make me believe. In fact, I believed all over again that God answers unified group prayer.

I shouldn't have been surprised. After all, in a series of parables about the unified, communal nature of his people, Jesus teaches that God answers group prayer. In his Gospel, Matthew records several stories about being humble like a child, seeking the lone lost sheep, restoring relationships through church discipline, and the dangers of not forgiving others. In the middle of teaching his followers to be a humble, forgiving community that values lost people and persistently reclaims offending believers with gentle confrontation, Jesus again promises limitless answers to prayer:

> Again, I tell you that if two of you on earth agree about *anything you ask for*, it will be done for you by my Father in heaven. For where two or three come together in my name, there am I with them.
> MATTHEW 18:19-20

Jesus puts a big spotlight on church unity when he tells us to pray together, and he promises power when we do. To emphasize the importance God places on unity when it comes to prayer, Jesus teaches the principle in the immediate context of instructions about resolving sinful conflicts in the community of faith. He gazes into the distant future and imagines his church as a peaceful community of followers lifting up their voices in perfect harmony. We get the English word *symphony* from the word translated "agree" in that passage. In the story of the Prodigal Son, that same basic word is used to refer to the music at the party the father throws for the son who has returned home.[1]

Jesus challenges us to offer a beautiful concerto of voices lifted together in one artfully unified petition. When God hears unified prayer, his heart soars like a music lover taking in a rapturous melody.

> **When Jesus hears unified prayer, his heart soars like a music lover taking in a rapturous melody.**

But it's music with a purpose! The word used to communicate "anything" in this verse is *pragmatos*, which means a deed or undertaking.[2] (It's also the source for our English word *pragmatic*.) The focus in this verse, then, seems to be on tangible, pragmatic deeds or undertakings.

With that in mind, I would render the passage like this: "If two of you on earth *harmonize* in prayer to ask about any *task*, my Father in heaven will make it happen for you." Jesus makes no promise here about making our own dreams come true. By saying "in my name" (verse 20), he clarifies again that the gathering must be for his purposes. When we pray together in unified community, centered on seeking lost sheep, Jesus shows up and moves among us in power.

Jesus also explained that bitter grudges erect a major barrier to unified prayer. He taught that we should never stand at the altar of prayer under the shadow of broken relationships. In Mark 11, when Jesus taught that God answers prayers of faith and faithfulness, he promised results with one limitation: "And when you stand praying, if you hold anything against anyone, forgive him, so that your Father in heaven may forgive you your sins" (Mark 11:25).

Bitter grudges erect a major barrier to unified prayer.

Does this explain some of the lack of power in our prayers? Are we clinging to resentment against anyone? Jesus implies that the static of ruined relationships hinders our prayers from being heard by God. If unified prayer attracts his pleasure like song, bearing a grudge strikes a sour note. Prayer offered in a room full of mutual resentment sounds like a repugnant cacophony to him. The next time you get together with your brothers and sisters in Christ, look around the room. Are there old wounds that haven't healed? Don't expect God to tune out the turbulence when we pray. He wants us to forgive one another and then agree in prayer. God searches for truly unified groups to bless with answers to prayer.

Our team in Papua New Guinea dreamed of building a facility where they could host their national coworkers when they needed to meet for training and translation work. So this group of missionaries began praying together, seeking direction about whether or not to take a leap of faith and begin building what they called the National Coworker Housing Project. Such an endeavor would require unprecedented funds; in fact, we had never raised money for anything like it in any of our fields.

First, the missionaries prayed about this project individually, using an idea called "listening prayer." They simply spent time praying about it and listening for God's leading as to whether or not he wanted the project to proceed. They prayed together in groups as well. Before long, they discovered that many of them had heard the same things while listening in prayer. Each of them prayerfully concluded that they should unite in faith to start the building, even though we did not yet have the resources to finance it. They even signed a contract with a builder.

Although we had made this facility the first priority of a major fund-raising campaign, I swallowed hard when I heard that the team had signed a contract obligating us to make the first payment immediately. I didn't know whether any funds had yet been donated for this project.

With some trepidation, I contacted our finance department and said, "We need $77,000 to start the building project in the Pacific area. What do we have in the account?" I almost fell over when I was told $64,000 had already been designated to it.

Even I can tell when God is answering prayer. I then asked our leadership team to pray over the weekend for the rest of the funds needed for that first installment. Normally, nothing comes in—at least nothing that's not already designated for another need. At that time, 97 percent of our giving was designated for a particular project or ministry. I had no reason to suspect that a major undesignated gift might spontaneously arrive in the mail. But I was impressed by the faith of these missionaries, and I had my suspicions that God had already provided.

During our daily staff prayer meeting that Monday morning, we prayed together for God to provide for this project. I walked away from the prayer time and found a small envelope in my mail slot. Inside was a handwritten note from a new donor accompanied by a check for $18,000! I wonder if God, knowing the surprise waiting just down the hall, was chuckling throughout our prayer meeting.

Everyone on our team was awestruck. The rest of the funds came in at the right time with a lot of work and prayer, and now that building bears fruit for God's Kingdom. This experience taught us to better understand the movement of God's power when we pray in unity.

To pray the kinds of prayers that Jesus promised to answer requires more than praying on our own. God moves in power as we harmonize together. Infighting hinders the power, but whenever we pray in concert, God's miracles multiply. God answers unified group prayer!

Questions for Reflection

1. Describe a time when you refused to forgive someone.

2. How did resentment impact your prayer life?

3. What is the likely consequence for your prayers if you don't forgive those who've wronged you?

4. Why do you think Jesus wants the church to "harmonize" in prayer?

5. How could you practice unified prayer in your church or ministry?

6. How could you spend time in your ministry or church praying for God to bring perfect unity and empower the members of the group to forgive one another?

7. What do you think would be the best way for you to provide your church or ministry with more opportunities for unified group prayer?

CHAPTER 6

FROM BOBSLED TO ROCKET

God Answers Specific Prayers That Build Faith

I TEND TO pray when I panic. Back in the middle of 2008 during the "Great Recession," I was starting to feel the financial heat like a droplet dancing on an electric burner. Then our ministry's financial report for July hit my e-mail in-box. My eyes just kept opening wider as I stared at the trend in the graph. For starters, our net revenue had been below zero every month that year, which I understand to be a bad thing financially. To double in size without increasing our income would ultimately lead to financial collapse. Worse, I couldn't help but notice that the last four months were on a perfect linear track toward tanking. We were taking a wild ride on a bobsled to insolvency.

But God had already taught me the perfect strategy to apply. I took one look at the January-through-July graph and wrote a half-page letter to my teammates worldwide. I tried to inspire them to pray by describing the incredible answers to prayer we had seen over the previous months.

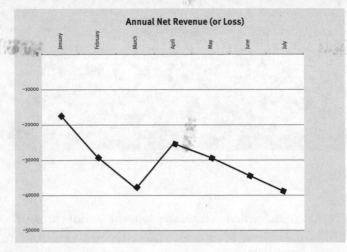

They were miraculous answers to issues for which we had united to pray regularly for a long time. After reporting that encouraging news, I penned this unremarkable request:

> *Please pray that God would pour out his blessings*
> *on our finances in general. Our general fund has*
> *been hit hard by the current economic climate. God*
> *is greater than the economy, and we know he will*
> *provide for his work. We also are cutting expenses*
> *here as much as possible.*

I knew there really wasn't any tangible place to cut expenses. I also knew I had precious little control over how much money would come in over the year. In short, financially speaking, without God we were toast.

Around the world, my teammates quietly approached the throne of grace on their knees. There is a quiet, beautiful simplicity to this strategy. Each member of the team has equal access to it. Everyone can bow before God, and only God can fully weigh its effect. No showmanship or bragging or posturing is possible. God's power works quietly among groups of faithful believers in ways we can't really see.

God's power works quietly among groups of faithful believers in ways we can't really see.

When I saw the end-of-the-year report, I knew God had heard our prayers. My eyes welled up with tears, and I silently studied the image in awe as the full impact of the fact that God answers *specific* prayers that build our faith hit me. If a financial expert were to analyze this graph, he or she would put their finger on the month of July and say, "What did you do right here? Whatever it was, you need to do a lot more of that." I searched in vain for a tangible explanation. I wanted to find trends to explain how it worked, so we could do it again. I never could understand how God did it. I just know he provided. All I had was God and prayer.

It's a little embarrassing and humbling to tell our auditors: "No sir, I haven't got a financial clue in the world why that happened." Ordinarily, I find that God works

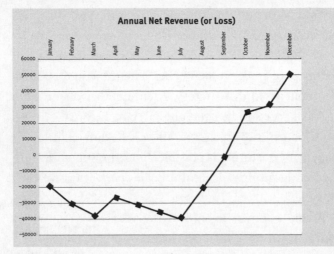

Annual Net Revenue (or Loss)

in subtle ways. He is invisible, after all. Some would call him mysterious. But when we pray specific prayers, we get powerful, obvious, and visible results that build our faith.

By applying prayer as our primary strategy, we were able to graph answers to prayer on a regular basis. In 2009 we applied the same strategy and ended the year with an overall income increase of 18 percent during the worst economic climate in decades. God has his own economy! Does the power of heaven build up behind a massive levee somewhere as God waits patiently for us to finally pray the kinds of prayers he promises to empower?

Jesus said that if you have faith, you can tell a mountain to go jump into the sea (Mark 11:23). That's a visible, measurable result. When a mountain hops up and does a cannonball into the ocean, we notice. Jesus wants us to pray for specific, conspicuous results.

Praying general prayers hinders our faith. Have you ever led a prayer by asking, "God bless the missionaries"? God could answer that prayer a thousand times, and we would never know it. It's not precise enough. Instead of commanding the mountain to cast itself into the sea as Jesus recommended, we are tempted to pray more generally, "God bless the mountains." God stands ready at our prayer times like a baseball player waiting for the right pitch. He longs for us to throw him something specific that he can knock out of the park. But we tend to hold on to the ball and murmur about blessings.

Praying general prayers feels safe because no one can prove that the prayer was not answered, but it makes for terribly dull prayer meetings. I wouldn't be surprised if even God has yawned his way through many prayers spoken in generalities.

Praying general petitions feels safe, but it makes for terribly dull prayer meetings.

This principle is really not all that surprising. After all, a lack of specific communication can be problematic in any relationship. Try talking only in generalities with your spouse and see how well *that* builds your relationship.

What would you like for your birthday?

"Just bless me, honey."

What would you like for lunch?

"I think I could really go for a blessing."

When should I pick up the kids?

"Oh, sweetie, your will be done."

It wouldn't take long to truly irk your spouse with that kind of talk. Likewise, God longs to genuinely relate with us about specifics, not generalities.

It's important to take time for praise, thanksgiving, and confession as we commune with God. But when the moment arrives for intercession, we need to be specific to keep our prayers powerful and engaging. Instead of praying for more people to come to church, pray for one hundred more people during the coming year. Instead of praying for God to make your congregation better at evangelism, pray for five or fifty or five hundred people to come to an evangelistic training course and commit to work in an evangelistic campaign over the next three years. At least by praying specifically, you will know whether or not God has answered your prayers.

Not every specific prayer needs to include numbers. We pray every day in our ministry that God would bring us to a state of perfect unity. We can generally see how that's going, even though we can't measure it using numbers. I've been praying for fifteen years that God would help us start a church in every major village among a people in West Africa who don't yet know Jesus. I can see progress happening over time. Because it's a specific prayer, I can see that God is answering my prayers. As a result, my relationship with the Lord is stronger, and I have much more interesting conversations with him.

When praying specific prayers geared to expand God's Kingdom, I have observed that it helps to frame the specific requests in terms of God empowering *believers* to achieve his mission, rather than praying for God to change the hearts of *unbelievers*.[1] For instance, I've seen far more answers when asking God to send believers to go out into the harvest field than when I've asked God to cause unbelievers to come to faith. It may be that God is not willing to infringe on the choice unbelievers have to rebel against him. I suspect that he freely commands those in his Kingdom, while leaving space to choose for those in rebellion against him.

I believe Jesus modeled this approach to prayer. When he saw the harassed and helpless crowds around him as he spoke and healed people, he encouraged the disciples to pray for workers: "Ask the Lord of the harvest, therefore, to send out workers into his harvest field" (Matthew 9:38). He did not pray, "God, cause these people to follow me."

Likewise, Paul often asked believers to pray that he would have the power to preach clearly and spot opportunities: "Devote yourselves to prayer, being watchful and thankful. And pray for us, too, that God may open a door for our message, so that we may proclaim the mystery of Christ, for which I am in chains. Pray that I may proclaim it clearly, as I should" (Colossians 4:2-4).

In another place he asked that people pray that the message would spread: "Finally, brothers, *pray for us* that the message of the Lord may spread rapidly and be honored, just as it was with you. And pray that we may be delivered from wicked and evil men, for not everyone has faith" (2 Thessalonians 3:1-2).

Notice that Paul wasn't asking for people to come to Christ, as we might expect. Instead, he asked for deliverance from the faithless and for power to make the gospel spread. He asked that believers might be moved to spread the faith, rather than for unbelievers to come to faith.

When the believers in Acts suffered opposition, they didn't pray for people to believe their message. Rather, they said, "Now, Lord, consider their threats and enable your servants to speak your word with great boldness. Stretch out your hand to heal and perform miraculous signs and wonders through the name of your holy servant Jesus" (Acts 4:29-30). They prayed that their testimony would be so bold and accompanied by such great power that they would accomplish their mission and that people would come to faith. To be sure, there are exceptions to this scriptural pattern,[2] but the main examples in Scripture lead us to pray for believers to grow in faith and ability rather than for unbelievers to respond.

In keeping with this model, I have found that the most powerful prayers to help unbelievers are oriented around praying that God would bring believers into their lives to testify powerfully about him. While other people may have had a different experience when asking God to produce faith in people, I have found that our Lord won't override the rebellious heart to force faith into an unbeliever, no matter how many years I beg him to do so. He will, however, command a believer to go to that person and then empower the Christian to testify with power that may break through the unbeliever's lack of faith. If you have persevered in prayer for a loved one to come to faith, I'm right there with you and don't think you should give up. Just make sure you are praying for God to reveal himself to him or her by calling many believers to join you in testifying about Jesus.

Note that in his final recorded prayer, Jesus said, "I am not praying for the world, but for those you have given me, for they are yours" (John 17:9). In praying specific prayers, we should focus on prayers asking God to empower his followers to accomplish Christ's mission.

Even as we pray that God's power would be evident in his people, we need to be specific. Why do we tend to pray with so little precision, anyway? Could it be that we pray broad, hesitant prayers because our faith is so fragile that it might waver if we discovered God didn't answer a specific prayer? That says more about our faith than about him. God wants to build our faith, but we make that difficult if we don't give him a chance to dazzle us with his omnipotence. We must make our requests explicit.

The great prayers of the Bible were specific. The Israelites cried out to God for deliverance from Egypt to the point that God told them to stop praying, and they crossed the Red Sea on dry land (Exodus 14:10, 15). When Joshua prayed for the sun to stand still in the sky until the battle was over, no one had to question whether or not God had answered; the sun just stood still (Joshua 10:12-14). Solomon prayed for wisdom (1 Kings 3:12), and God made him so wise that "people came from all the nations to hear the wisdom of Solomon" (1 Kings 4:34, NRSV). When Elijah "prayed earnestly that it would not rain," the answer was obvious to every thirsty person in Palestine because "it did not rain on the land for three and a half years" (James 5:17).

God wants to build our faith, but we make that difficult if we don't give him a chance to dazzle us with his omnipotence.

God has infinite power, so what you pray and how you pray matter. After that, the actions you take that are consistent with your prayers will bear more fruit. Think of the opportunity that would have been lost if Jesus had stood before Lazarus's tomb and prayed, "God, bless my friend." Instead, after praying to his heavenly Father, Jesus said, "Lazarus, come out!" (John 11:43). One minute Lazarus's body was bound tightly to rot in the dark of the tomb. One prayer later he was sauntering out of the tomb and provoking such a revival of faith that the authorities began plotting to kill him and put him back in the tomb.[3]

As God began answering our prayers for more teammates, we quickly figured out that we would need a new building for our headquarters to supplement our portable modular facility.

At first we prayed that God would provide another modular building, which would cost about $350,000. Not only had we never raised that much money for a single project before, we still owed money on our first modular unit. We were worried.

Trying to be a good leader, I came up with a plan to take baby steps forward. That made perfect sense from a human standpoint. I remember someone in a board meeting saying, "That's the most sensible plan I've heard."

That felt good. I thought we should keep our plans within the realm of reason. But even this doable plan scared us, and we kept saying to each other, "How will we ever raise so much money?"

Our whole team prayerfully entered into our building campaign, only to find that the sensible, humanly possible modular option was not coming together. We could not make that plan work. Obstacles and roadblocks popped up at every turn. When we inquired about leasing the land next to our current modular, the owner drew up a new lease arrangement calling for a huge increase in rent for the land. We could not justify the increased monthly expense. It turned out that God had much bigger plans.

We were forced by circumstances to take a bigger leap

and purchase property where we would build a permanent facility. At the beginning of the project, I listed all the potential showstoppers for this course of action. My knees shook on a regular basis as I prayed for help.

We ended up purchasing and developing twenty-two acres and building a beautiful five-thousand-square-foot office building. During the three-year project, we made a conscious effort to persevere in specific, unified group prayers of faith that were consistent with all Jesus' name represents. It ended up costing far more than we ever could have imagined. In hindsight, I realize we did not know the things we needed to know in order to develop the property. The whole course of action could easily have ended in disaster. But it's in my new office in that very building that I am writing this chapter.

Jesus was right! God really does answer *whatever we ask* when we pray the kinds of prayers that Jesus promised he would answer. "Now to him who is able to do immeasurably more than all we ask or imagine, according to his power that is at work within us, to him be glory in the church and in Christ Jesus throughout all generations, for ever and ever! Amen" (Ephesians 3:20-21).

The extreme prayer that Jesus prescribes is the kind that stalks up to a mountain and gestures an imperious finger toward the ocean, knowing that God's power will prove sufficient. What mountain stands in the way of your family or church? What peak needs to be leveled for your ministry to advance or for you to impact your workplace for Christ? Don't just murmur generalities! Get down on your knees and pray something unequivocal, because God answers specific prayer. Once you see one obstacle removed, your faith will be strong enough to bulldoze a hill. Once the hill rolls aside, you won't be so reticent to pray down a peak. No godly work will be impossible when you pray specific prayers that build your faith.

Questions for Reflection

1. Discuss a time when God answered prayers that you prayed. How specific were those prayers?

2. Why do you think God reacts differently when you pray specific prayers as opposed to general prayers?

3. What has caused you at times to hesitate to pray specific prayers?

4. What precise prayers do you think your church or ministry should be praying right now? What impossible things need to happen for your ministry to really make a difference in your community?

5. How can you shape your prayer requests to more closely follow the biblical example of praying for God to empower believers rather than centering

your prayers on praying for unbelievers to respond to the message?

6. Make a specific prayer list designed to help your church or ministry overcome mountains and obstacles in order to make a great impact on your neighborhood, your workplace, and the world.

CHAPTER 7

FORSAKEN

God Answers Faith-Filled Complaints

Just when I think I understand God's open-ended promises about prayer, something happens to show me that God will not be contained within the boundaries that make sense to me. He's not at all a safe, predictable God.

At the same time Pioneer Bible Translators was experiencing unprecedented answers to prayer, my friend Chris was devastated by a crisis in his own life. Chris had gone to East Africa as a Bible translator, only to be forced to return because he was suffering from debilitating chronic fatigue syndrome. His maturity and understated strength of character inspired our whole team. His quiet spirituality was magnetic. Upon his return to the States, he became our team's prayer coordinator because, even though he was exhausted physically, he could still lead the charge in prayer.

The irony was not lost on any of us that God chose to leave Chris physically weak while Chris himself challenged us to pray with ever-increasing powerful and miraculous results. And so we fasted and prayed for Chris and his family. We laid hands on him and spoke against demons. We used any other prayerful approach we could imagine.

One day Chris and another coworker came to my office. Our hearts were sick and tired of fruitless prayer for our weary brother. We couldn't just fold our hands and pray courteous prayers anymore. We had watched, awestruck, as God had answered prayer after prayer. From our limited viewpoint, we wondered how God, in good conscience, could refuse to help his child in this dreadful season of his life. The three of us got down on our knees and drew from the riches of a long-standing tradition in Scripture—one that is often brushed aside in our culture. As we prayed together, we quoted the basic thrust of every prayer of complaint in Scripture we could remember.

Have you ever felt like complaining to God? If so, you might resonate with these powerful protests from Jeremiah:

> God, you tricked me, and I fell for it.
>
> JEREMIAH 20:7 (MY PARAPHRASE)

> You are always righteous, O LORD,
>   when I bring a case before you.
> Yet I would speak with you about your justice.
>
> JEREMIAH 12:1

How could God tolerate such direct confrontation from Jeremiah? And what about Job's painful questions?

> I will not keep silent;
>> I will speak out in the anguish of my spirit,
>> I will complain in the bitterness of my soul. . . .
> When I think my bed will comfort me
>> and my couch will ease my complaint,
> even then you frighten me with dreams
>> and terrify me with visions,
> so that I prefer strangling and death,
>> rather than this body of mine.
> I despise my life; I would not live forever.
>> Let me alone; my days have no meaning. . . .
>
> If I have sinned, what have I done to you,
>> O watcher of men?
> Why have you made me your target?
>> Have I become a burden to you?
> Why do you not pardon my offenses
>> and forgive my sins?
> For I will soon lie down in the dust;
>> you will search for me, but I will be
>>> no more.

JOB 7:11, 13-16, 20-21

Job is saying, "God, if you won't heal me, at least leave me alone!" Is that okay? And is it okay to accuse God with words from Habakkuk like these?

> How long, O LORD, must I call for help,
>   but you do not listen?
> Or cry out to you, "Violence!"
>   but you do not save?
> Why do you make me look at injustice?
>   Why do you tolerate wrong?
>
> HABAKKUK 1:2-3

Did you know that such words were in the Bible? If so, do you wonder whether we are actually supposed to say them? Won't God get angry with us for daring to complain like this?

One year when my team and I were translating the Old Testament in West Africa, we happened to be working on Job and Jeremiah at the same time. The local translator on the project paused one day and floated a tense question: "It seems to me that these men and their constant complaining to God would eventually make him angry. Is it okay to complain to God?"

The answer came to me in a flash. "God can tolerate our complaints," I said. "Complaining to God is allowed with one major condition: we must continue to faithfully obey and follow him in spite of our suffering." That's why the complaining and grumbling of the Israelites in the wilderness aroused the cataclysmic anger of the Lord (for example, Numbers 11:1-3), but Jeremiah's and Job's complaints did not. In the face of agony, these two men never stopped loyally serving God. Their complaints demonstrated that they had faith— they offered faith-filled complaints. The Israelites' grumbling, on the other hand, was a demonstration of faithlessness.

Complaining to God is allowed with one major condition: we must continue to faithfully obey and follow him in spite of our suffering.

The New Testament contains examples of this same principle. Paul implored God to remove his suffering: "There was given me a thorn in my flesh, a messenger of Satan, to torment me. Three times I pleaded with the Lord to take it away from me" (2 Corinthians 12:7-8). Yet Paul came to accept his pain as God's way "to keep [him] from becoming conceited" (verse 7) after he experienced indescribable supernatural visions and revelations.

Even Jesus experienced the pain of unanswered prayer. The night before he died, he prayed passionately, "Abba, Father, . . . everything is possible for you. Take this cup from me" (Mark 14:36). As he was dying on the cross, Jesus drew from one of the great prophetic complaints of the Old Testament (found in Psalm 22) as he cried out, "My God, my God, why have you forsaken me?" (Matthew 27:46).

Jesus had the faith to fulfill the prophecy, yet he would not deny the reality of the suffering involved. He showed his faith by reflecting on Scripture and having the courage to live out the fulfillment of that prophetic psalm. If relying on biblical, faith-filled words of complaint is okay for Jesus when he suffered, it's okay for us too.

Jesus and Paul didn't put a sunny, Christian facade on their suffering. There was no hollow, false perkiness at the Cross. They proved that complaints and faith are not mutually exclusive.

Complaints and faith are not always mutually exclusive.

Yet too often insincere cheerfulness is a hallmark of Christianity as it's practiced in the United States. Sometimes we assume that if we are suffering, we must be doing something wrong. Actually, biblical Christianity allows for the keening wail of a suffering complaint when the desolation of this world overwhelms us. Sometimes the only faithful response to the torment we see around us is to cry out for an answer from the only one who has sufficient magnificence and glory to set it right—and to bring justice to this fallen creation.

Sometimes the only question that makes sense to us is, how long? Sooner or later our lives will come to that point where we echo the psalmist's question, "My soul is in anguish. How long, O LORD, how long?" (Psalm

6:3). The time will come when the martyrs' question in Revelation will resonate with our soul: "How long, Sovereign Lord, holy and true, until you judge the inhabitants of the earth and avenge our blood?" (Revelation 6:10). For the moment, God's answer—to "wait a little longer" (Revelation 6:11)—fails to quiet the craving in our souls. Great faith is required to patiently watch and prayerfully wait upon the Lord.

Scripture illustrates ways God answers our grievances. When Job was subjected to all kinds of torment through no fault of his own, he felt justified in launching his objections to God, scandalizing his pious friends. Finally, when the hollow philosophy of those men could not soothe Job's soul, God answered Job's demands with his own barrage of inquiries:

> Job, do you know how to create a cosmos? Do you help mother deer give birth? Where are you when I make thunder and lightning? Do you have a clue how to run this world? Brace yourself, because I'm going to ask you my questions and see if you are still interested in getting the answer to your complaints.
>
> (MY PARAPHRASE OF JOB 41)

In the face of God's glory and omnipotence, Job relents: "Surely I spoke of things I did not understand, things too wonderful for me to know" (Job 42:3).

When Jeremiah complained, he received this answer: "If you have raced with men on foot and they have worn you out, how can you compete with horses? If you stumble in safe country, how will you manage in the thickets by the Jordan?" (Jeremiah 12:5).

Essentially God was saying, "Jeremiah, are you already complaining? This is only chapter 12. You have forty chapters of misery to go! You think this is hard now? You have no idea how strong I can make you."

Likewise, in answer to our complaints, God tells us, "You think you can't take it anymore, but I have only begun to create in you the full measure of your strength of character. You have only just begun to fully reflect my glory. I'm making you into an unassailable fortress that can withstand anything this world throws at you."

Even as Jesus asked, "Why have you forsaken me?" from the cross, the words of the rest of Psalm 22 must have reverberated in his place of torment: "Future generations will be told about the Lord. They will proclaim his righteousness to a people yet unborn—for he has done it" (Psalm 22:30-31).

When Paul pleaded for relief, God answered: "My grace is sufficient for you, for my power is made perfect in weakness" (2 Corinthians 12:9). God answers faith-filled complaints with grace, with character development, with power to persevere, and with a long-term plan that makes all things turn out right in the end.

As far as I know, God's answer to complaints has never fully satisfied anyone on this ruined planet. It's never fully quenched our thirst. All creation groans along with our own hearts in anticipation of the day when we will shed this temporary dwelling and penetrate the portals of paradise. That's why Jesus puts his own answer to our complaints at the very end of the Bible: "Yes, I am coming soon" (Revelation 22:20).

> **God answers faith-filled complaints with grace, with character development, and with the power to persevere.**

Frustrated, unrealized expectations are a part of our faith experience. In extolling the beauty of faith-filled people throughout history, the writer of Hebrews observes, "These were all commended for their faith, yet none of them received what had been promised" (Hebrews 11:39). In the face of blunt disappointment in this dark world, the complaint has its place, as long as we are unrelenting in our faithful obedience.

As for my brother Chris, he has no victory story to tell yet. Eventually even the strain of coordinating our prayers was too much, and he had to resign from our mission. It makes me cry to think about it. We still don't get it. There is no relief from some misery on this earth. There is just faith-filled complaint, in which we pour out the ache of sadness like a drink offering before God. How long, O Lord, will you wait?

We will not be able to truly evaluate how God has answered our prayers until Jesus' return. One day every knee will bow to him and every tongue confess him (Romans 14:11). We who overcome will sit down with God on his throne (Revelation 3:21). He will uncover the truth about our intended nature, our real identity (Revelation 2:17). At that time, we will know fully the things that baffle us today (1 Corinthians 13:12). We will be with him as his children (Revelation 21:7). On that day, I imagine our Father taking us aside and explaining it all. We will feel the caress of the Carpenter's calloused, nail-scarred hand as he wipes away every tear from our eyes. Finally the sobbing will stop, the mourning will cease, and the sorrow will be lifted from our hearts. Christ will make all things right for each one of us.

Until that moment, we have only the comfort of lifting up our faith-filled complaint to the one who has broad enough shoulders to bear the burden for us. As we seek the fulfillment of Jesus' promises to answer our prayers with infinite power, we need to honestly approach him and admit when we are upset by his silence.

His final answer does comfort me after all: "'Yes, I am coming soon.' Amen. Come, Lord Jesus."[1]

Questions for Reflection

1. When have you been overwhelmed by pain in spite of your desire to be joyful as a Christian?

2. What are you currently experiencing that makes you want to complain to God about unanswered prayer?

3. How does God answer complaints in the Bible? How do those answers make you feel?

4. How might praying psalms of complaint help you process your own questions?

5. What do you think it will be like to finally have your tears wiped away by Jesus?

CHAPTER 8

MARCHING ORDERS

Extreme Prayer Maximizes Jesus' Prayer Promises

FOR ME, the most exciting aspect of basing ministry on prayer is watching the people I work alongside grow in faith.

Earlier I explained how our recruitment efforts seemed to stall in 2010 after we had added a large number of new missionary candidates for several consecutive years. Even though I figured it might be God's way of protecting us from growing too fast, my team and I continued to pray. I was blown away at how God answered our prayers and filled all the slots, but I was also humbled and encouraged by the response of a colleague. Take a look at his e-mail:

From: *Nathan*
Date: *June 17, 2010*

*Three weeks ago, our worldwide team began a
prayer fast asking God to send us more workers for*

his mission. At that time, we had ten recruits for the year and another twelve individuals who had verbalized that they wanted to join Pioneer Bible Translators in the near future. While these twenty-two lives are nothing short of a demonstration of God's grace, I felt deep within my soul that God wanted to do something more.

During this time, I had this gnawing feeling that God was holding back more responses so that we wouldn't be confused about who was truly responsible for recruiting workers for God's harvest. I shared with my teammates and my Sunday school class that I felt God was going to do something in such a way that he and ONLY he could be given credit and worship. If you remember, three weeks ago I also asked YOU to join us in asking God to unleash his Spirit upon this ministry and bring the people into this work who would extend his glory unto all the earth.

It is my joy to tell you that in the last three weeks, GOD has brought us twenty-seven ADDITIONAL responses to our prayer requests! Praise his holy name! Praise him.

I don't know if these numbers do anything for you, but my heart is simply full of love and joy right now for the people behind these commitments. Each one of these special people represents God's faithfulness and God's workings amongst his people. These people represent the continuation of Jesus' Great Commission and an extension of God's story. These dear people actually believe that God is real. They believe that he meant what he said when he said that he would "never leave us or forsake us." While many of them are still full of fear, have doubts, and have many questions about how God is going to work it all out—they have stepped out in faith and said, "God, I'm all in!"

In case you can't tell, my heart is also full of gratitude unto our God. God knew that if he'd sent these people to us earlier, we couldn't have handled it. He also knew that if he'd sent these people to us earlier, he wouldn't have received the full praise and glory that he deserves. Praise his name!

Following the strategy of extreme prayer has taught our entire ministry team how to believe in God's power and publicly call others to that belief. Did you notice the elements of extreme prayer represented in Nathan's e-mail?

> He prayed about the "extension of God's story." In other words, he asked for things consistent with *Jesus' name* for "the master's business."
> He told his Sunday school class *in faith* that he believed God was about to move.

> He explained that, because God waited until we *persevered* in prayer, we knew that the credit and glory all belonged to God.
> He sent out e-mails to his whole community of partners so they could pray together *in unity*.
> He prayed *specific prayers* that built the faith of everyone who heard about the answers.

In other words, Nathan was firing on all the pistons of extreme prayer.

By the way, Nathan might have chosen to take a lot of credit for those amazing recruitment results. He was the person spearheading our recruitment efforts then. Yet I don't catch a whiff of pride in this e-mail. If we had not been fasting and praying for years for this to happen, Nathan might have been tempted to take credit. Because we had been practicing these principles of extreme prayer, Nathan didn't boast; he believed.

Practicing the principles of extreme prayer leads to belief, not boasting.

What about you? Are you in a position to see God begin to do "whatever you ask"? Begin by considering, *What am I doing as part of God's plan for the world and in Jesus' name? What am I working on that only God can do and that benefits only his Kingdom? In what ways am I striving together with my family, church, or ministry for God's glory?*

If the answer is nothing, you won't be able to access

Christ's promises—not really. Yet Jesus invites you to open yourself to the limitless possibilities that come when you offer the kinds of prayers he promised to answer. And when you faithfully unite with others to persist in group prayer for specific endeavors consistent with his character and plan, God's power will far surpass your imagination.

How can you know and be about your "master's business" (John 15:15)? By now, you should realize that no special knowledge or abilities are required. I do, however, want to pass along some of the strategies I've learned through my own adventures in extreme prayer:

1. **Begin by asking God to show you what he wants you to do.** Read the Bible and imagine what would change, both where you live and around the world, if you were to operate by the values of the Kingdom of God. You might consider:

   Who around you lives far from Jesus?
   Whom do you see suffering oppression and overwhelming need? How can you reach out to them?
   What part can you play in fulfilling Jesus' commission to teach all the people of the earth to follow him and obey his commands?
   What are the impossible things that must happen for you to minister in the Kingdom?

What unattainable goal would make a difference
in your community for Jesus' sake?

Once you have an idea of what ministry in his
Kingdom God has given you, you have something
to pray about that can access the power of his
promises.

2. **Listen for God's assignment.** There is freedom
   in the realization that you are not responsible for
   doing everything that seems urgent. Rather, like
   Jesus, you do only what you see the Father doing.[1]
   Extreme prayer will help you realize you no longer
   need to strive so hard to please other people; with
   directions from God, you can concentrate on doing
   only what he shows you to do. When you ask him
   to guide you, God will reveal the critical work that
   will enable you to make the greatest impact.

   I have learned that if I follow God's instructions
   for just a few hours each week, I accomplish more
   than I do in a seventy-hour workweek of my own
   design. Suddenly prayer isn't a peripheral obliga-
   tion; it becomes my only hope to save time, to suc-
   ceed at leadership, and to avoid burnout. Intimacy
   with God becomes the well I draw from for the
   strength and direction I need in order to lead.

   If you find yourself on the verge of burnout

in ministry, relax. Stop doing what people expect you to do. Begin investing time each day to discover what God wants you to do. Breathe a little. Working harder for longer hours is not going to solve your problems. Rather, work smarter by getting God's direction and power.

3. **Keep strategic prayer lists.** First, compose a list of those who count on you for spiritual guidance. Who are the people you influence? Are you a mother? A company CEO? A nursery worker? An engineer? An elder? No matter who you are, God has placed people in your life to nurture and strengthen.

    After writing down their names, begin praying for things in their lives that are consistent with the name and character of Jesus. Begin to keep a written list of your "master's business." Since these are people you know, it's usually not hard to list ways in which God can make their character more godly. You may know struggles they have physically that prevent them from achieving the work that God has given them. I have prayed for years that my children would do well in school and that God would prepare just the right spouse for them. I have prayed that God would give them a great mission in the world.

As you pray for people you lead, you will know specific ways that God could use them more powerfully to accomplish their part of the mission of your church or ministry. Usually I pick a Scripture that I think would bless them with greater power, and I regularly pray that Scripture for them. For example, you might choose parts of Leviticus 26:6, 9-12:

> I will grant peace in the land, and you will lie down and no one will make you afraid. I will remove savage beasts from the land, and the sword will not pass through your country. . . .
>
> I will look on you with favor and make you fruitful and increase your numbers, and I will keep my covenant with you. You will still be eating last year's harvest when you will have to move it out to make room for the new. I will put my dwelling place among you, and I will not abhor you. I will walk among you and be your God, and you will be my people.

If you don't know what else to pray, repeating the promised blessings of Scripture over someone can be an inspiring guide.[2] Keep that list with you through the day and lift those people up as you have the opportunity.

Praying for the people under your influence will provide them with critical support. Moses modeled this in the way he backed up Joshua during a critical battle. When Joshua went out to fight, Moses climbed a mountain to pray over the situation. "As long as Moses held up his hands, the Israelites were winning" (Exodus 17:11). Whenever Moses became too exhausted to pray and his arms fell to his sides, the enemies of God's people began to win. Whatever your ministry—whether you are a mom or a dad or an elder or a preacher—you will find a similar dynamic.

After praying for those you influence, begin praying through a second strategic prayer list, which you develop in cooperation with your ministry or church group (see item number 4). As you pray through both lists, ask God for his daily marching orders with regard to these people and ministries. Ask him what he would have you do as he works through you to be part of the answers to these prayers.

4. **Get together regularly with others in your community of faith for unified, persistent group prayer.** Your second strategic prayer list contains God's directives for your church and ministry as it seeks to access the power of Christ's "whatever you

ask" promises. Fill it with specific requests so you will be inspired to pray regularly, particularly as you track God's responses to your prayers.

To achieve unified group prayer, gather with the people in your sphere of influence so you can call upon God once a week or every morning. If you have a family, you can begin with your children. (Some people call this "family devotions," but at my house we refer to it as "family commotions.") Maybe you can lead your Sunday school in more extended, intentional times of prayer. If you are an elder, incorporate extreme prayer into your elders' meetings. If you lead a ministry team, begin each day with strategic prayer in your office. Teach the people on your team to tap into all the prayer principles taught by Jesus.

Be sure to carefully guard the unity of the group by encouraging them to forgive each other whenever the need arises. Thank God for each answered prayer and celebrate each response. When God leaves certain prayers resolutely unanswered and you cannot understand why, lift up a faith-filled complaint.

Nothing in our lives will ever be the same as we pray these kinds of prayers, because Jesus keeps his promises!

5. **Pray expectantly.** If you find your mind wandering away from prayer because of anxieties, concerns, or a pressing workload, don't feel guilty. Don't assume you are bad at prayer. Work with your thoughts. The Holy Spirit may be pointing out what you need to pray about. Lift up to God every anxiety that enters your mind. When you start thinking about a person you know, cry out to God on his or her behalf. As you pray through the worries that surface in your mind, your prayer times may even grow longer and sweeter, bringing greater peace.

Our lack of faith may be subtle, but we can expect God to paint a big red *X* on it when we begin praying. When I first practiced extreme prayer, I quickly learned that praying for direction from God without having a pen and paper at hand is a flashing neon sign of faithlessness. If I really believed that God would answer by giving me work to do, I needed to be prepared to write down his instructions. Once I began bringing a pen with me to my prayer times, I quickly filled the margins and backs of my prayer lists with to-do lists. But these weren't like the lists I would make for myself without prayer. With this list, I found myself efficiently crossing items off as they actually got done! God tells me what to do as I pray to him *in Jesus' name*. Prayer becomes like downloading instructions from God.

Early on, I stumbled over another sign of my lack of faith. When I began praying with our team, I created a "long-term" prayer list. I assumed our requests were so difficult it would take God a long time to answer them. After a year or so, I found God answering prayers so quickly that I could not keep the list up to date. I thought, *Oh yeah, nothing is too difficult for God. I knew that.*

Prayer becomes like downloading instructions from God.

That's when I began calling it our *strategic* prayer list. Gradually, as we have seen missionaries recruited, Scriptures translated, and challenging sums of money raised, our whole team has grown in faith. By now we have seen so much answer to prayer that our dreams have grown ridiculously large. After all, Jesus said "whatever you ask."

In fact, I suspect that Jesus made these blank-check promises not only to advance his Kingdom, but also to increase our trust in him. He asked the question himself: "When the Son of Man returns, how many will he find on the earth who have faith?" (Luke 18:8, NLT). Extreme prayer is Jesus' design to ensure that there really will be faith on the earth when he comes back. He will find it in you and me as we learn to pray extreme prayers.

I can't wait to see the joy on Jesus' face as he returns to the earth to discover men and women of faith all over the planet. I pray he will catch you and me radiating faith in every action we take.

Questions for Reflection

1. What is the first step you will take this week to apply the principles of extreme prayer in your own life?

2. How will you promote and practice prayers *in Jesus' name*?

3. How will you promote and practice prayers of faith and faithfulness?

4. How will you promote and practice persistent prayer?

5. How will you promote and practice unified group prayer?

6. How will you promote and practice specific prayer to build faith?

7. How are you prepared to emulate the faith-filled complaints in Scripture?

8. How can you combine all these principles of extreme prayer to maximize your Kingdom impact?

NO LOITERING

I STILL REMEMBER that day back in 1995 when I stomped off into the African bush, almost ready to quit the mission and get a divorce. I thank God that my wife and I were able to focus on prayer, experiencing the help and then the transformation we needed. Now the West African language community with whom we were working has the full Bible translated into their language. There was only one small church back in 1995, but now there are several, and those are working to multiply.

Since 2007, when we began leading our mission with the strategy of prayer, God has dramatically grown our team and helped us overcome great financial and personnel challenges. When we started emphasizing extreme prayer, our team was translating the Bible for 9 million people speaking 35 languages in 5 countries. Six years later, we translate for at least 26 million people speaking

60 languages in 14 countries. We see a great movement of the Holy Spirit around us.

We have looked back at these answers to prayer and asked, "If God can do that, what is impossible for him?" With that reasoning, the board of our mission just approved a goal to start and finish 250 translation projects by 2050, concentrating on filling the gaps in the Bible translation movement. If we can complete what amounts to more than 10 percent of the remaining translation projects in the world, we estimate that our many great partner agencies will be able to finish the translation task in the coming generation.

Oh, I know—our goals are humanly impossible. I get that. But Jesus has already provided the strategy. We will pray the kinds of prayers he promised to answer with unlimited power. I can't wait to see what happens!

Over the past twenty years, I've been convicted by my natural tendency to focus on my own story instead of the story God wants to write in my life. My prayers, like those of many people, have at times centered on relationships, health problems, and personal decisions. I wanted to know if my life would turn out to be a tragedy, a comedy, a romance, or an action adventure. My prayers were really a request that God make my story into what I dreamed it should be.

I now know that from his heavenly vantage point, Jesus doesn't view prayer that way. He challenges us to lift up our eyes to a higher understanding of our purpose.

God's epic plan features an invisible plot and powerful unseen antagonists. In this story, Jesus is the hero, and we are all challenged to abandon our roles as incidental extras loitering about the set and take on speaking parts as supporting actors.

There are cataclysmic clashes and casualties. It's unlikely that any of us will make it out alive, and no one will escape unscathed. All around us unseen bullets ricochet, and lives are devastated in the heat of the unnoticeable battle. Our eyes are closed to the spiritual narrative unfolding around us, but deep down we all are dimly aware that some poignant drama unfolds on this earth. At the core, God's story is not about action adventure. A beautiful romance is unfolding daily as God courts each person, patiently working his plan in history. He is tying up all the loose plot complications into a happily-ever-after tale of his design. Jesus gets his bride in the end. His Kingdom really does come. His will really is going to be done on earth and in heaven.

Jesus made unlimited promises about prayer to entice us into God's story. He works through us to prove to countless unseen spiritual spectators that he is infinitely wise, uniquely beautiful, and matchlessly magnificent. He intends to provoke a plot twist in our story so astonishing that a standing ovation will break out among the angels even as the demons begrudgingly confess his glory with a final shudder.[1] Jesus' promises about prayer are a whispered invitation to enter the grand story of his triumph.

If you pray consistently, you will tend to overcome the challenges you face. If God's power isn't activated through prayer, your life will tend to fall apart. Both in the way he lived his life and in his teachings, Jesus challenged us to develop a prayer life balanced by the elements in the acronym ACTIVE. Our prayer should include adoration, confession, thanksgiving, intercession, and prayers to vanquish our unseen enemy. Yet at some point, we are to take our prayer life to the world-changing level Jesus intended by applying the principles of extreme prayer.

Jesus made unlimited promises about prayer to entice us into God's story.

I leave you with a final example that comes straight from Scripture. Consider the lessons we learn as we see how God worked when the first believers applied Jesus' principles of prayer and changed the world around them:

God answers prayers made in Jesus' name. Peter said, "Through faith in the name of Jesus, this man was healed—and you know how crippled he was before. Faith in Jesus' name has healed him before your very eyes" (Acts 3:16, NLT).

God powerfully answers prayers fueled by faith. "A deep sense of awe came over them all, and the apostles performed many miraculous signs and wonders" (Acts 2:43, NLT; see also 3:6; 9:40; and 16:25-26).

God answers persistent prayer. "They all met together and were constantly united in prayer" (Acts 1:14, NLT).

God answers the prayers of those who meet and pray in harmonious unified groups. "[Peter] went to the home of Mary, the mother of John Mark, where many were gathered for prayer" (Acts 12:12, NLT). God miraculously released Peter from prison in response to his fellow believers' prayers—in fact they were still praying when Peter arrived to tell them what had happened. (See also Acts 2:1; 2:42-44; 13:2; 20:36; and 21:5.)

God answers specific prayers. "Publius's father was ill with fever and dysentery. Paul went in and prayed for him, and laying his hands on him, he healed him" (Acts 28:8, NLT; see also 4:29-30; 9:40; and 12:5).

God accepts our complaints when we continue to walk in obedience. After the Jewish leaders warned Peter and John never to speak to anyone in Jesus' name again, the apostles told the other believers about the council's threat:

When they heard the report, all the believers lifted their voices together in prayer to God: "O Sovereign Lord, Creator of heaven and earth, the sea and everything in them—you spoke long ago by the Holy Spirit through our ancestor David, your servant, saying,

> 'Why were the nations so angry?
>   Why did they waste their time with futile
>   plans?
> The kings of the earth prepared for battle;
>   The rulers gathered together
> against the LORD
>   and against his Messiah.' . . .

> "And now, O Lord, hear their threats, and give us, your servants, great boldness in preaching your word."
> ACTS 4:24-26, 29 (NLT)

Their prayers were answered with power:

> After they prayed, the place where they were meeting was shaken. And they were all filled with the Holy Spirit and spoke the word of God boldly.
> ACTS 4:31

Not only did that place of meeting shake, but the whole world has been trembling ever since. Even the Pharisees who had launched the threats were begrudgingly impressed: "When they saw the courage of Peter and John and realized that they were unschooled, ordinary men, they were astonished and they took note that these men had been with Jesus" (Acts 4:13).

When those ordinary men and women who trusted God left that humble prayer meeting, they changed the kingdoms and nations that had been raging against them. Within a few hundred years, the emperor himself believed in Jesus. All over the world, cultures and peoples have had their values upended and reordered. Whole nations have been founded on the ideals of Jesus and his followers. The aftershocks of that prayer meeting continue to ripple across the earth. Now that's what I call extreme prayer!

We may be ordinary people, but because Jesus promises to answer our prayers, we will do "even greater things than these"!

The same Jesus who sent them into the world also sends us! When we apply Jesus' promises about prayer, others will note that we, too, have "been with Jesus." He promises to answer our prayers, no matter how extreme they appear. We may be unschooled and ordinary people, but because Jesus promises to answer our prayers, we will do "even greater things than these" (John 14:12)!

God does not turn away from us when we pray about our strategies, but he wants us to make prayer *the* strategy. Will he really do *whatever we ask*? Anything? Will we leave behind our shaken lives and begin instead to shake up the whole world? Will we seek his power to break our addictions, aspire to greater holiness, transform whole cities, stop wars, revolutionize cultures, and even bring God's Kingdom to every people group on earth? I know only one way to find out.

I dare you to try it.

Questions for Reflection

1. What change do you hope extreme prayer will make in your life, ministry, or workplace?

2. List one or two of the most important things you've learned about God and his purpose, as well as about yourself and your purpose, as a result of reading this book.

3. How might you help other people you know learn to pray the kinds of prayers that Jesus promised to answer?

I WROTE THIS book because I wanted to share the most important thing God has taught me. But he used other people to teach it. Thank you so much to all who had a hand in this book!

To my parents, who taught me to pray: thanks for the hours of patience and the brilliant example! Thank you for showing me the value of Scripture and the importance of reaching out to others with God's Word. I never need to go far to see an example of unshakable faith. Special thanks to my mother, who helped me process and improve the whole manuscript. Thank you for always working with me on my homework above and beyond the call.

To my wife, Rebecca—where to begin? Your character and persistence drew us into the ministry of Bible translation. It became our dream, but you dreamed it first. Thank you for adopting my passion to teach Jesus to those who follow the Qur'an. You made our twelve years in a rural village the greatest time of my life! You made our family and our home lovely in the midst of rugged surroundings. Thank you for remaining the romantic enigma I will never solve, the beautiful mystery that never fails to fill me with irresistible curiosity and passion.

To Max Lucado, who mentored me spiritually and taught me to preach by example: thank you for making Jesus more vivid and relevant to me. Thank you for being the greatest model of humility I have encountered. Thank you for writing the foreword and lending your credibility to me.

To Brad and Estel Willits, who showed us the way: thank you for all the guidance you have given in your lives.

To my predecessor in leadership, Rondal Smith: thank you for showing that strong leaders must begin in prayer. Thank you for proving by example that leaders can thrive spiritually their whole lives without falling into burnout or scandal.

To Mandy Chankin, who helped me form the original shape of this work and asked the penetrating questions that led me to write chapter 7: thank you for being kind while you stretched my thinking.

To Dot Drulman, who helped inspire me to begin this book: thank you for correcting my writing.

To Jim Akovenko of The Seed Company, whom God used to help me connect with Tyndale House Publishers: thank you for quickly valuing my work and getting me in touch with exactly the right person.

To Kim Miller, the editor who helped me get my amorphous thoughts into a form people can read and understand: thank you for helping me be clear.

To my colleagues at Pioneer Bible Translators: thank you for inspiring me every day to grow in my faith!

To those of you who read this book: thank you for being patient with my attempts to explain what God has taught me. I pray that God will use these limited words to release his unlimited power in your life.

Endnotes

INTRODUCTION: SHAKEN BUT NOT STIRRED

1. 2 Chronicles 16:9
2. Lamentations 3:22-23

CHAPTER 1: BLANK CHECKS

1. I first heard the phrase "Prayer is the strategy" while serving with InterVarsity Christian Fellowship.
2. I was inspired by the memory of a sermon about unanswered prayer that Max Lucado gave while I was in college. In his message, he went systematically through a lot of Scriptures about prayer.
3. If you're interested in reading more about prayer and spiritual warfare, I recommend the book *The Devil Goes to Church: Combating the Everyday Attacks of Satan* by David Butts (Terre Haute, IN: PrayerShop Publishing, 2009).

CHAPTER 2: NAME POWER

1. John 11:35
2. Revelation 7:17; 21:4

CHAPTER 3: BLIND TRUST

1. Except in the case of the demons, mentioned in James 2:19.
2. The Hebrew word *aman* has as one of its meanings "made firm." It can even refer to a solid structural support like a pillar (Francis Brown, S. R. Driver, and Charles A. Briggs, *A Hebrew and English*

Lexicon of the Old Testament [Oxford: Clarendon Press, 1951], 52). The word for *faithfulness* is based on this same root word. Therefore, believing in an unseen truth means understanding that it's firm and stable and then taking action that relies on this truth. For example, God promised offspring to Abraham, and "Abram believed the Lord" (Genesis 15:6). As a result, he entered into a covenant with God. In Exodus 4:31 the people "believed" and so bowed down in worship. In Jonah 3:5, because the people of Nineveh "believed," they fasted. The same basic dynamic happens in the New Testament Greek in Hebrews 11, where the people affirmed for their faith took great action on the basis of what they believed. Some Christians today believe that intellectual assent to the facts of the Bible can replace faithful discipleship. As the passages above illustrate, that's not the way the biblical idea of faith and belief works. So when Jesus challenges us to pray in faith and believe, his idea likely includes a call to being faithful and reliable.

3. 2 Corinthians 4:7
4. John 9:3
5. 2 Corinthians 5:1-5
6. John 16:33

CHAPTER 4: SHAMELESS
1. See Luke 11:1, 5-13; 18:1-8.
2. This treatment is widely needed by people living in rural Africa. See http://www.worldconcern.org/44centcure/.

CHAPTER 5: THE SYMPHONY
1. Luke 15:25
2. Barclay M. Newman Jr., *A Concise Greek-English Dictionary of the New Testament* (Stuttgart, Germany: United Bible Societies, 1971), entry 4968.

CHAPTER 6: FROM BOBSLED TO ROCKET
1. I first heard the idea of "believer-centered" prayer in a devotional presented by an InterVarsity Christian Fellowship staff member more than twenty years ago.

2. Acts 26:29; Romans 10:1; 1 Timothy 2:1-4
3. John 12:10

CHAPTER 7: FORSAKEN

1. Revelation 22:20

CHAPTER 8: MARCHING ORDERS

1. John 5:19
2. Other Scriptures you might pray for someone include Deuteronomy 28:3-13; Matthew 5:3-11; 1 Corinthians 12:8-11; 1 Corinthians 13:4-13; Galatians 5:22-23; Ephesians 6:10-20; and Philippians 3:1-11.

CONCLUSION: NO LOITERING

1. Ephesians 3:10

About the Author

GREG PRUETT HAS been president of Pioneer Bible Translators, based in Dallas, since January 2007. Before that, Greg, along with his wife, Rebecca, and their three children, lived in West Africa for more than twelve years, where they completed a translation of the entire Bible into the Yalunka language and shared Christ's love with people who traditionally follow the Qur'an. Greg continues to oversee church-planting efforts among the Yalunka through cell phone contact with their church leadership and by yearly visits to West Africa. He has a degree in civil engineering from Texas A&M, as well as an MA and a PhD from Fuller Theological Seminary. He also has linguistic training from the University of North Dakota and the Graduate Institute of Applied Linguistics.

Online Discussion *guide*

TAKE *your* TYNDALE READING EXPERIENCE *to the* NEXT LEVEL

A FREE discussion guide for this book is available at bookclubhub.net, perfect for sparking conversations in your book group or for digging deeper into the text on your own.

www.bookclubhub.net

You'll also find free discussion guides for other Tyndale books, e-newsletters, e-mail devotionals, virtual book tours, and more!